# Great

# Scots!

Scottish Men Whom Shaped,
Changed and Created the Modern
World.

By

Jason M. Fonseca

*To Mary*
*I hope*
*you enjoy the*
*historic journey*

Front cover photographs: Glamis Castle, personal collection, taken in 2012. Photograph of author, personal collection, taken on London Tower Bridge in 2012. Flag of Scotland Saltire, public domain, because it consists entirely of information that is common property and contains no original authorship. MacDonald of Ardnamurchan tartan STA ref: 3275 Crown copyright. Source; the Scottish Register of Tartans. Front and back cover design: Darian Trama. Second printing..

First published in 2014 by Jason M. Fonseca

Copyright © 2014 by Jason M. Fonseca

ISBN: 978-0-9912128-0-4

Printed in the United States of America.

This book is dedicated to my wife Luz, and my two sons;
Justin and Joshua. To my mother Kathleen McDonald Fonseca and my
father Manuel Fonseca, for your never-ending, unconditional love. To my
brother Darren, for your inspirational seeds of wisdom throughout this
journey.


Grateful acknowledgment is also given to the following persons, who have
given me encouragement and assistance throughout this journey:
my cousin Melissa, my cousin Danny, my Aunt Margaret,
Professor Malcolm Baird and James Goodfellow.

# Table of Contents.

Introduction                              1

Acknowledgment                            2

Alexander Graham Bell                     4

John Logie Baird                          12

Andrew Cummings                           20

John Loudon McAdam                        24

John Boyd Dunlop                          30

Kirkpatrick Macmillan                     36

Sir Robert Watson-Watt                    40

James Goodfellow                          48

Adam Smith                                54

Sir Sandford Fleming                      60

James Watt                                66

William Murdoch                           76

Sir Alexander Fleming                     82

Sir James Whyte Black                     88

Professor Dr. Ian Donald                  94

Alexander Muirhead                        100

Sir James Young Simpson                   104

Dr. Alexander Wood                        108

James Lind                                112

Andrew Carnegie                           118

| | |
|---|---|
| John Napier | 128 |
| Alexander Shanks | 132 |
| Thomas Robb Coughtrie | 136 |
| Arthur James Arnot | 140 |
| George Bruce | 144 |
| Samuel Wilson | 148 |
| Declaration of Independence | 152 |
| Sports & Athletics | 154 |
|     Shot Put | |
|     Weight Throw | |
|     Hammer Throw | |
| Curling | 158 |
| Football | 162 |
| Andrew Watson | 166 |
| Golf | 170 |
| Jim McCormick | 174 |
| Hugh Nicol | 179 |
| Lawrence Tynes | 184 |
| Bobby Thomson | 188 |
| References | 192 |

# Introduction

It is said Rome was not built in a day and so can be said of our modern society. From how we communicate with each other to how we spend our recreation time, all was once just a thought in someone's mind. During the process of conducting research for the book a captivating question began to consume my thoughts. Who were the people who imagined and then created all the different facets of our modern world? Their origins repeatedly began to center on a stretch of land surrounded by the North Sea and the Atlantic Ocean, Scotland.

This is a story that stretches across time and age. Whose roots traveled over the oceans and in its path touched the lives of millions throughout the world.

As most people born in New York City, they themselves or at least their families derived from somewhere else in the world. My family is not any different. My father's ancestral roots derive from Puerto Rico and further back from Spain. But that is for another book. This book's journey will travel to Scotland and my mother's ancestral lineage.

# Acknowledgment

My inspiration for writing this book derived from many places. I remember as a young boy my father exposed to a song titled *Black Man* written by Stevie Wonder. I was also inspired by two books *Black Profiles in Courage: A Legacy of African-American Achievement,* written by Kareem Abdul-Jabbar and *The Good, the Bad, and the Mad: Some Weird People in American History,* written by E. Randall Floyd. But the preeminent motivating force emerged from traveling to the William Wallace Monument in Stirling, Scotland the summer of 2012. Climbing the two-hundred forty six step spiral staircase I entered the Hall of Heroes room on the second floor. In the room along with the busts of sixteen of the most influential Scotsmen of all time sat a list of inventions credited to Scottish men that changed the modern world. Truly awe-inspiring! Looking to further my knowledge of who these men were? I asked the curator at the entrance of the museum if there was a book I could read to gain more of an insight on who these men were. He said there was no such book, as of yet. Well there was my spark.

The other reason I decided to write this book is selfish in nature. Most people in the world want to know who their ancestors were and where their families derive. I am not any different. This book is dedicated to the people who inspired, molded and created our modern society with their imagination and genius.

*"A life is not important except in the impact it has on other lives."*

An excerpt from *I Never Had It Made: An Autobiography of Jackie Robinson* (1972) by Jackie Robinson and Alfred Duckett.

*"Individuals of genius show the way, and set the patterns, which common people then adopt and follow."*

William James, philosopher.

Alexander Graham Bell.

"Courtesy of the Parks Canada/Alexander Graham Bell National Historic Site."

## Alexander Graham Bell

Inventor of the Telephone, the first devise ever created that successfully carried the sound of speech over electrical wire.

Walk down any street in any town or city throughout the world and within a few moments you will soon see someone approaching from the opposite direction nose down in their phone. The telephone and its subsequent advancements have given the human race the potential to be connected to anyone and everyone living on the earth, as long as you have their telephone number. This is a brief account of how it all began.

Alexander Graham Bell was born on 3 March 1847, in Edinburgh, Scotland. At birth he was not given the middle name Graham by his parents. His middle name was later added to distinguish himself from his father, Alexander Melville Bell. His mother's name was Eliza Symonds Bell. She was Alexander's first and most influential teacher in his life. Mrs. Bell began to go deft shortly after Alexander's twelfth birthday. Being very close to his mother, he helped her develop a basic signing system of tapping each others figures. This allowed Mrs. Bell the ability to communicate with her family and the outside world. Though she was hearing impaired, she was able to decipher some sounds with the use of a speaking tube. Bell's grandfather, uncle and father all worked in the field of elocution.

Elocution is the study of visual speech. Due to young Aleck's Scarlet Fever affliction much of his primary schooling was completed at his home on 16 South Charlotte Street in Edinburgh. On those rare occasions when he was well enough to attend classes he was enrolled at the Hamilton Place Academy followed by the Royal High School of Edinburgh. As a student at these fine institutions he acquired a great interest in the sciences especially biology. Regrettably due to heavy absenteeism young Aleck could only achieve minimal passing marks. In 1862, at the age of fifteen he moved to London to live with his grandfather for a year. At sixteen years of age he secured employment at the Weston House Academy in Elgin, Moray, as a pupil-teacher of elocution and music. During his time at Weston he also attended classes in Latin and Greek. For his services as a pupil-teacher he was compensated with free board and £10 per session he completed. The following year 1864, he enrolled at the University of Edinburgh. In 1868, he was accepted into the University of London. In 1870, soon after his brothers, Edward and Melville, died of Tuberculosis, twenty-three year old Alexander and his family left the shores of Scotland on the SS Nestorian and immigrated to Brantford, Ontario, Canada.

Though he always referred to himself as a teacher of the deaf, Bell soon became enveloped in the pursuit to improve upon several inventions initiated by some of his contemporaries. One of these early inspirational contemporaries was Samuel F.B. Morse and his 1837 invention of the Electric Telegraph. The way the Electric Telegraph

6

operated was by sending a message across a wire to a receiver by means of an electric pulse. Each pulse or series of pulses represented a different letter of the alphabet. The drawback of this technology was that the process of converting the pulses to letters then to words then to sentences was a very arduous. Another one of Bell's inspiring contemporaries was Leon Scott. In 1851, he invented the Phonautograph. The way this devise operated was by having someone say a word into the mouthpiece. The vibrations on its inner-membrane would cause a lever to vibrate across a pane of smoked glass, hence making a picture of the human voice. Bell was intrigued with this technology because it reminded him of the inner-workings of the human ear. Insight from these two inventions and others of the time gradually drove Bell to the invention of the telephone.

On the night of 10 March 1876, the first telephone call was made. With Bell and his partner Thomas Watson in rooms fifteen feet away the message was transmitted. Bell had the transmitter while Watson had the receiver. As written in Thomas Watson's autobiography the first message sent was, "Mr. Watson, come here, I want you!" But in reality the message might have been slightly, just possibly modified from what was historically recorded. As the story goes, Bell had just accidently spilled battery acid on himself while making the call to Watson. Subsequently, as I and probably many of the readers of this book can attest profanity at times and moreover in times of great stress can flow out of a Scotsman mouth quicker than a New York minute. Thus, what was truly said during that momentous first transmission might, perhaps be forever lost to posterity?

7

Soon after that memorable first call Bell and Watson perfected the telephone. They then headed to Washington D.C. to acquire a patent for their new invention. On 7 March 1876, Alexander Graham Bell was issued patent #174,465. This was the first US patent issued for the telephone. In August of the same year the first long distance call was made. Bell's father made the call from his home in Brantford Ontario to Bell who was in a store in Paris Ontario eight miles away. In the years to follow the pair of Bell and Watson would perform numerous demonstrations of their new invention around New England and eventually for Queen Victoria of England. 10 November 1882, was another momentous day in the life of Alexander Graham Bell. This was the day he became an American citizen.

One of Bell's greatest personality traits was that he never rested on his past accomplishments or achievements. He was always in pursuit of the next improvement, the next invention. These are several examples of some of his less memorable inventions that lead up to his telephone. The Multiple Telegraph was one such machine. It allowed multiple messages to be sent simultaneously, thus allowing for a reduction of costs for sending a telegraph and thus increasing productivity. In addition, it gave Western Union some unsolicited competition. Another invention was the Autograph Telegraph. The technology behind this invention was that it recognized the sender's hand-writing then sent the message. Another invention of Bell's was called the Photophone. This was the predecessor to the modern cellular telephone. The way this machine operated was a beam of light would carry the human voice rather than it being carried through a wire. Bell was also involved with the basic theories behind magnetic recording, the predecessor to cassette tapes, floppy disks and hard disks. He was also one of the earliest contributors to the recording of the human voice. Bell also held a world record for ten years. It was for his HD-4 Hydrofoil. In 1919, he set the world marine speed record of 114 km/h (70.86 mph). He was also one of the founding fathers of the National Geographic Society.

Another invention Bell was involved with was called the Vacuum Jacket. This was a project Bell sporadically toiled with from as far back as 1881. The Vacuum Jacket was the predecessor to the iron lung invented in 1927 by Philip Drinker and Louis Agassiz Shaw. The primary function of this invention was to alleviate the suffering of polio victims. It was widely used until the polio vaccine was developed in the early 1950's. Another invention was the Bullet Probe, the predecessor to the X-Ray. When the President of the United States, James Garfield was shot in the back near his spine and arm on 2 July 1881, Bell was commissioned by U.S. government officials to invent a devise to aid the President in his grave condition. The crude contraption was constructed out of batteries, coils and wires. The premise behind this instrument was for it to be placed above the affected area. Then when the instrument would vibrate this would indicate the location of the bullet. Regrettably several factors prevented it from successfully locating the President's bullet. It was later discovered that while examining the President the apparatus detected a rather abnormally large infected area.

9

The reason behind this occurrence was later reveled; the apparatus was detecting the metal from the bed springs in addition to the President's bullet. Unfortunately, President Garfield passed away on 19 September 1881, sixty-nine agonizing days after being shot. The autopsy reveled Bell did not in any way attribute to the President's rapid demise. In addition, due to the location of the bullet it would have been virtually impossible for Bell's probe to detect the bullet. The cause of death was proven to be infection caused by the constant probing of doctors with their unsanitized fingers into his wounds.

  At this time the production of the telephone began to erupt with great volume and velocity. "In 1880, there were 50,000 telephones in the United States. By 1890, there were 250,000 telephones. By 1900, 800,000 people had telephones." Jarnow, James pg. 27. By 1915, the American Telephone and Telegraph Company (AT&T) had built 130,000 telephone poles across the United States, hence connecting the country from coast to coast with telephone wires. To commemorate the momentous event the executives at AT&T decided it would be great for publicity if the creators of one of the world's most renowned inventions would make the first transcontinental telephone call. For twenty-three minutes on 25 January 1915, Bell in the AT&T head office on 15 Dey Street, New York City and Watson on 333 Grant Ave. in San Francisco, spoke to each other. Near the end of the conversation Bell paraphrased to Watson what he said to him all those years ago during their first telephone call, "Mr. Watson come here, I want to see you." Watson then replied;"Mr. Bell, I will, but it would take me a week now."

10

On 2 August 1922, the father of the telephone Alexander Graham Bell died with his wife at his side, at the age of seventy-five in his Beinn Bhreagh Estate on Cape Breton Island, Nova Scotia, Canada, from complications brought about from Pernicious Anemia and Diabetes Mellitus. On the day of his funeral all telephone transmissions were halted for one minute throughout North America in remembrance to the father of the telephone.

It is estimated there are roughly seven and a half billion active cellular telephones in the world today. That means there are more active cellular phones than there are people living on the earth. It is also more astonishing there are far fewer toilets, an estimated four billion on the earth.

"The inventor is a man who looks around upon the world and is not contented with things as they are. He wants to improve whatever he sees, he wants to benefit the world; he is haunted by an idea. The spirit of invention possesses him, seeking materialization."
Alexander Graham Bell, 1891.

John Logie Baird.

"Courtesy of Malcolm Baird and www.bairdtelevision.com."

## John Logie Baird

Born on 13 August 1888- Died 14 June 1946

He is recognized as the inventor of the television. But more accurately he is the inventor of the first televised moving images in 1926.

The life of John Logie Baird began very modestly in Helensburgh, then part of Dunbartonshire, Scotland. John was born in his family home affectionately called, "The Lodge" at the intersection of Argyle Street and Suffolk Street. He was the fourth and youngest child born to Reverend John and Jessie Baird. His path to formal education took several stops throughout his life. Baird attended primary school at Larchfield Academy, which was then part of the Lomond school system. He then attended Scotland Technical College, now called the University of Strathclyde and finally to Glasgow University. Unfortunately due to the outbreak and aftermath of the First World War, he never graduated with a college degree. The creation of the television did not have a very auspicious beginning. The concept of capturing a moving image and subsequently transmitting it through the air incrementally evolved through numerous streams of thought, error and even the occasional explosion. Some of the early patriarchs that preceded and inspired Baird in his development of the television were Paul Nipkow, Lee de Forest and Arthur Korn. Paul Nipkow patented the first electromechanical television system he called the Elektrisches Teleskop in 1884, though regrettably he never built a working model.

Lee de Forest and Arthur Korn's technical preoccupations surrounded the development of amplification tube technology. In addition to these three technicians there was also a Scottish scientist named Alan Campbell Swinton, who assisted in trudging the television into existence. In 1908, Swinton wrote a letter to the journal *Nature* in which addressed the newly discovered properties of electrons. Within his letter he detailed the technical concepts behind an electrical television in which would be operated with the use of cathode ray tubes. Though expensive to construct Swinton was convinced his concept could and would be built in the near future. Even though his ideas were only theoretical in nature, they must have planted the seeds of possibilities within Baird's own imagination.

With help from these ambitious technological undertakings, time was gradually pushed to the date of Tuesday 26 January 1926. This is widely recognized as the day the first working mechanical television system was publicly demonstrated. The demonstration took place in Baird's laboratory and residence at 22 Frith Street in the Soho district of London. It was witnessed by over forty honored members of the Royal Institution and newspaper reporters from *The Times* that recorded the event for posterity. It is rather incredible to realize at the time of Baird's first television demonstration only one out of every one thousand people in Britain owned a radio, so conducting a television demonstration was a rather mind blowing phenomenon. Through these first television images produced by Baird's

Televisor were shown on a screen no larger than a business card consisting of faint choppy outlines and shadowy grainy images, they provided the television the ability to step out of the realm of myth and into reality and the possibility of producing a viable working television. The television would soon transform how people throughout the world were entertained and informed within just a few decades. Soon after this initial demonstration Baird established the first television broadcasting company accurately titled the Baird Television Development Company LTD. His newly formed enterprise broadcasted out of the Crystal Palace of London comprised of a ten-kilowatt power station, had the ability to transmit images of rather good quality within a thirty mile radius. By the 1930's a British or Western European, could buy Baird's Televisor for approximately eighteen pounds. Within the years 1929 to 1932 about three thousand television enthusiasts took Baird up on his offer and enjoyed transmissions of popular singers and comedians broadcasted periodically by Baird Studios in conjunction with the BBC.

Soon after developing his first mechanical television comprised primarily of scavenged parts, a bicycle lamp, a knitting nettle, a hat box lid, cardboard, string, and a coffin lid as a base, he soon invented other machines that would soon change the face of the modern world. One of these inventions was called the Phonovision. This was initially called the Television Record and Replay System. The way this machine succeeded in recording moving images was with a wax disk that had the ability to be replayed. This was the world's first video recorder.

15

Another invention was called the Noctovision. This machine utilized infer-red lighting to allow Baird to film in the dark. The way this apparatus worked was by having the user sit inside a shed while the subjects were outside in the open air. He soon proved this method of lighting was much easier on the subjects compared to his earlier intensely hot lighting systems. He also proved this instrument had the ability to detect reflective radio waves, hence the ability to detect distant metallic objects. With the help of time this technology would later be developed by other Scotsmen into RADAR. His next technical feat of significance occurred on 9 February 1928. From a short-wave radio station in Coulsdon, London, Baird successfully transmitted the first television images across the Atlantic Ocean to Hartsdale, New York. On the third of July of that same year Baird conducted his first demonstration of a primitive mechanical color television. This feat of genius was conveyed through three separate colored filtered disks of red, blue, and green, simultaneously transmitting identical image in rapid succession onto a 3X5 viewing screen. He also created the world's first three-dimensional television that same year he called Stereoscopic Television. The first successful public demonstration of Stereoscopic Television took place in Baird's Laboratories in Long Acre on 10 August 1928, for an audience of distinguished audience of scientists and press. The one drawback to this technology was the viewer of his Stereoscopic Television needed to wear cardboard glasses with one red lens and one green lens in order to witness the images properly.

As the popularity of Baird's television increased and his broadcasting network grew, he decided to venture to New York City to share his technology with the New World. In September 1931, Baird sailed to Manhattan in the attempt to reach an agreement to broadcast television events in New York City. While in New York he met up with the founder, owner and broadcaster of WMCA radio station Donald Flamm. His stations had exclusive broadcasting rights to every event held at Madison Square Garden, boxing matches, hockey games, bicycle and running events as well as theatrical events. Unfortunately, Baird's progressive fate lied in the acquisition of a broadcasting license from the Federal Communication Committee in Washington. Regrettably after three months of anticipating a positive response from the FCC his request was denied. As eloquently illustrated by Donald Flamm, "They didn't want a Foreigner spearheading television in America." Soon after this unfortunate set back he soon returned to the British Isle to expand upon his television ventures throughout the United Kingdom. In 1932, he put his reputation on the line and self-funded the worlds first live, outside television broadcast. The event that was given this momentous honor was the world famous Derby horse race at Epsom Downs. This race is Britain's most prestigious annual horse race.

In a perpetual state of financial woe throughout the Second World War, as the War was coming to an end by 1944 Baird focused his attention more vigorously towards the worlds first all electric, high definition, three-dimensional, color television receiver. Baird desired his new technology to be delivered by one thousand line resolutions, serviced by an International Worldwide Television Broadcasting Service. After suffering from a stroke in February 1946, his work-load dramatically became diminished. His last official project pertaining to television was the coordinating of the Second World War victory parade in July of that same year.

Regrettably on 14 June, John Logie Baird, the father of the television, passed away in his sleep at his home on 1 Station Road in Bexhill-on-Sea, Sussex, England at the age of fifty-seven.

Throughout his lifetime Baird received one hundred seventy eight patents for his inventions, most notably for the first Electromechanical Television System on 15 January 1929: US1699270 and the patent for the first Color Television System on 5 September 1933: US1925554.

The human race will forever be gratefully indebted to John Logie Baird for his unwavering drive and creative initiatives that created and developed such a powerful, world-altering machine.

Side bar fact:

It is estimated there are roughly one and a half billion television sets presently in operation on the earth.

"Courtesy of Malcolm Baird and www.bairdtelevision.com."

Late 19<sup>th</sup> century sanitary water closet and drainage, 1888-1889.

Popular Science Monthly Vol. 34.

## Alexander Cummings

Inventor of the flush toilet.

If there was an imaginary line between a
civilized and uncivilized society, that boundary line would undoubtedly
lie across the flush toilet. This single contraption would do more to rid
the world of such diseases as Cholera, Dysentery, Typhus and Typhoid
Fever than any pharmaceutical could ever remedy. Archaeological
evidence has proved the world's first latrine-like plumbing system was
built on the Orkney Islands some ten thousand years ago. Crude drainage
systems leading from stone huts to nearby streams have been discovered
throughout the islands. These crude discoveries allowed the residence of
the islands the luxury of relieving themselves indoors instead of outdoors
in the cruel Scottish winter air. A multiple of creative minds throughout
the ages have placed their fingerprints on this life essential devise. One
of these ingenious minds was John Harrington and his privy for Queen
Elizabeth I. As the years passed, the word "John" would become
synonymous with the toilet. Contrary to popular belief it was not Thomas
Crapper who first received a patent for the flush toilet. The recipient of
this distinguished accolade goes to a watchmaker named Alexander
Cummings. He was born in Edinburgh, Scotland in 1733 and died on
Tuesday, 8 March 1814 in London, England at the age of eighty-one.
Cummings received patent #814 for his flushing water closet in 1775. A
water closet simply is a room with a toilet and a sink. The essential
features that separated Cummings invention from its contemporaries was

the addition of a water trap inside its copper bowl. In addition to the usage of an S-shaped pipe that prevented sewage gases from escaping into the residence. Throughout his lifetime Cummings made his profession as a mathematician, mechanic and watchmaker. He was also an appointed Fellow of the Royal Society. One of the primary responsibilities of the Royal Society was as scientific advisor to the British government.

It is difficult to imagine a world without the flush toilet. Cities throughout the world during Cummings lifetime were filthy, dingy places to reside, to say the least. With no sewage system in place the inhibitors of tenements would go about discarding their waste and excrement by simply throwing it out a window. If you happened to be walking on the street at that exact lucky moment you would probably hear a cry of, "Gardy Loo" from above. This is a direct variation of the French phrase, "Gardez L'eau" which loosely translated means, watch out for the water. But it was not water being thrown out of those windows. After hearing the warning cry you would holler back, "Hold your hand". This hopefully would give you ample time to get to the wall prior to the deluge. Remnants of this practice can still be seen when a gentleman walks along a walkway with a female companion, proceeding closest to the street, farthest from the wall.

With time modifications were made to the loo. In the late eighteen hundreds Thomas Crapper came along with several improvements to the commode. He invented the pull chain for greater flushing capacity and an air tight seal between the commode and floor.

He also made improvements to ventilation systems that carried sewer gases through an opening in the residences roof. He also teamed up with a pottery maker named Thomas Twyford to create the first porcelain toilet. The improvements to the flush toilet alleviated many of the unsavory odors in the residencies of the time which were unfortunately common place throughout Great Britain up until the late eighteen hundreds. In addition to reducing the probability of highly explosive bacteria carrying fumes from entering the homes of the cities dwellers. These public sanitary breakthroughs in time also assisted in improving Britain's cities water supplies thus enabling their cities the ability to increase their population capacities. Due to these social improvements, in 1848 the Public Health Act of Great Britain was enacted. It stated all newly constructed dwellings should be built with some sort of indoor toilet.

Side bar facts:

The Scott Paper Company sold the first roll of toilet paper in 1879 in Philadelphia. Toilet paper became common place during the first decade of the 1900's.

The St. Andrews Paper Mill of Great Britain invented the two-ply toilet paper in 1942.

Pomegranates combine with cloves were the worlds first attempt at a toilet air-freshener.

Furthermore, the reason people shake hands using the right hand is because it is customary to wipe with your left.

John Loudon McAdam.

## John Loudon McAdam

Reformed road construction with his revolutionary development called Macadamization.



If one was about to commence with the arduous task of constructing a city its arteries and veins would undoubtedly be its roads. The concept of paved roads is as old as the concept of city construction itself. Archeologists have discovered evidence of paved roads in many of the Sumerian and Babylonian early city states. The Romans were the first to fashion a functional road system throughout their empire. Though unfortunate, the massiveness of the Romans road system infrastructure provided it with many difficulties to maintain. From the fall of the Roman Empire during the fourth century until the late seventeenth hundreds there were not many technological advancements pertaining to road construction. Not until John McAdam arrived with his new ingenious construction concepts that would transform the face of Great Britain and the world.

John Loudon McAdam was born into minor-nobility, the youngest of ten children on Tuesday 21 September 1756 in Ayr, Scotland. He was the only surviving male from the Waterhead family lineage. His mother's name was Susanna Cochrane, the niece of the 7th Earl of Dundonald. His father's name was James McAdam. His father's connections to the Bank of Ayr granted him a life of affluence. But tragically he lost most of his wealth due to bad investments.

As a child, young John attended the parish school of Mr. Doick's at Maybole near Blairquhan. When John was fourteen years of age his father passed away. In his will he wished his young son to be entrusted to live with his uncle William MacAdam in New York City. John soon began a stewardship at his uncle's counting house. When the American Revolution erupted the McAdam clan sided with the British Loyalists. Envisioning a profitable opportunity he became a government contractor engaged in the sale of confiscated war prizes, either land or goods. This was an occupation that materialized from the upheavals of war. The title used for this line of work was an agent of prize. When the American Colonies were declared the victors of their Revolution the political climate of McAdams' New York began to change. Due to their loyalist allegiance, John and his family, his wife and two young children, were not welcome in America anymore. So they soon moved back to Scotland. Though he amassed a considerable fortune while living in the colonies he had to relinquish all his property and most of his assets when he left the New World. He was only allowed to leave with enough wealth to purchase an estate in Sauchrie, Ayrshire, when he arrived back in Scotland.

In 1783, soon after returning home from his stay in the American Colonies he began to orchestrate repairs to the roads surrounding his estate. Observing the uneven, soil-based roads continuously getting muddy around his property, he soon arrived at the

26

realization there must be a better, more efficient way to construct his estates surrounding roads. The first step in McAdam's construction process was to crown the road to allow for proper drainage. Then large boulders and rocks were set on top of a natural sub-soil to form a durable foundation. Men would sit on small stools breaking the rocks with small hand-held hammers. They would break larger granite rocks into smaller uneven stones to be tightly packed between the larger rocks to help with drainage. The weight of horse drawn carriages and coach traffic would gradually smooth the road surface. This process would later be called Macadamisation within road construction circles.

Due to his first-class road construction, he was offered and accepted the post of deputy lieutenant and road trustee of Ayrshire in 1783. In 1789, he was named Navy food supplier. In 1798, John and his family moved to Bristol, England. In 1803, he began to work for the Board of Works in Bristol. By 1815, he was appointed Bristol's Surveyor-general of the Road Trust. In 1819, he wrote and published a book on road construction: *A Practical Essay on the Scientific Repair and Preservation of Roads*. His follow-up publication in 1820 was titled: *Present State of Road making.* In 1827, he was appointed general surveyor of metropolitan roads of Great Britain.

Modifications by Thomas Telford refined upon McAdam's road construction technology. His primary contribution was to raise the center of the road to allow for better drainage and by arraigning the stones that would be placed on the surface by shape and thickness. This process allowed for better longevity and smoothness of the surface of the road. This process was the forerunner to using bitumen; a tar based binding material that eventually evolved into tarmacadam on black top roads. The first tarmac road was laid in Paris in 1854. With the invention of the steamroller in 1866, McAdam's roads would be able to be laid with more effectiveness and with less expense.

Towards the end of his life he was offered the prestigious title of knighthood by the Royal Crown. But due to his advanced age he declined the offer and passed it to his son John. He died on Monday 26 November 1836 in Moffat, Dumfrieshire, of a heart-attack at eighty years old. He was laid to rest next to his grandmother. John McAdam's ingenuous road development altered the waves of commerce and travel, while transforming the landscape throughout Great Britain and eventually the world.

Till this day the term Tar-Mac is used to describe airport runways.

"Public Domain. Courtesy of Carl Rakeman, artist. This image is a work of a U.S. Department of Transportation employee, taken or made as part of that person's official duties. As a work of the U.S. federal government."

John Boyd Dunlop.

"Courtesy of Dumfries Museum."

## John Boyd Dunlop

Inventor of the commercially viable Pneumatic Tyre.

John Dunlop was born on Wednesday 5 February 1840, in Dreghorn, North Ayrshire, Scotland. Anthropologists have discovered artifacts that exhibit evidence that Dreghorn is believed to be the oldest and in continuous use settlement on the British Isle. John was born into a modest farming family. At nineteen years of age he was accepted into and attended veterinary college in Edinburgh. The institution is presently part of Edinburgh University popularly known as the Dick Vet. It was named after its founder, William Dick. After graduation he worked in Edinburgh for around ten years within the field of veterinary surgery. After getting married in 1867, he moved to Belfast Ireland. While living in Ireland Dunlop established a rather large veterinary practice for himself. Though one of the drawbacks of such a large practice was the traveling to patients homes and the rough, uneven roads of Ireland did not help in the matter one bit. That brings us to a crossroads where the needs of a changing world eclipsed the technology of the time.

The wheel, perhaps the greatest invention of all time did not have many if any technological advances for nearly four thousand years. Carriage wheels of the late nineteenth century did not conform to the road. The passenger felt every bump, pebble and twist as the coach lumbered down the causeway.

31

Wheels in Dunlop's day were either manufactured out of iron or wood, held together with spokes or solid rubber. Unfortunately none of these alternatives gave any relief to the passenger. The story of the Pneumatic Tyre began very modestly on May Street in Belfast in 1887. Dunlop's son had a tricycle with solid rubber wheels which was very uncomfortable to ride, difficult to steer and unfortunately unable to produce much speed. As the complaints came in from his son John and as any good father would do, Dunlop tried to fix his son's little problem. Always an inventor at heart Dunlop began to tinker away in his workshop, trying to figure how to create a more effective wheel. After some time he came up with the idea for the Pneumatic Tyre. A Pneumatic Tyre is a type of tyre with pressurized or compressed air inside. This technology would provide a much needed cushion between the bumpy road and riders on their bicycles, coaches or motor vehicles. It would also reduce wear and tear on the rims of the wheels themselves. His newly created Pneumatic Tyre made their first public appearance in May of 1889 when Willie Hume, the captain of the Belfast Cruisers Cycling Club became the first person brave enough to used Dunlop's Pneumatic Tyres on his bicycle while competing in the Queen's College Sports Races. Resulting from his unmatched confidence in Dunlop's Tyres and his athletic prowess, Hume was victorious in all four cycling circuit events at Queen's College that year. Later that same year he nearly matched those results in Liverpool by winning three out of four of their circuit races. Soon flocks of bicycling enthusiasts began to covet a pair of Dunlop Tyres. With this new found interest in his invention, Dunlop set forth to patent his creation. He was issued patents for his Pneumatic Tyres from the United Kingdom on 8 March 1889 # 111116.A9 and from the United States on 9 September 1890 #US435995 A.

Unaware another Scotsman named Robert William Thomson patented a similar idea for a pneumatic tyre forty-four years prior in 1845, two years after being issued his patents Dunlop was informed that they were deemed invalid. The reason behind why Thomson's concept never totally caught on at the time was due to the high manufacturing cost of his tyres. In addition, since automobiles were not yet invented and petal bicycles were a fairly new invention in their own right the demand for Thomson's tyre was just not there yet. Later that year Dunlop and his partner, William DuCros founded the Dunlop Pneumatic Tyre Company and began to manufacture the first commercially viable pneumatic tyre in Belfast, Ireland. In only three years Dunlop's tyre factories opened up on the mainland of Europe. In the twenty years to follow, the pneumatic tyre was taken around the world and the Dunlop Tire and Rubber Corporation became the first global multinational company to sell and manufacture tires worldwide. Standing at the precipice of the automobile age of the late nineteenth century, John Dunlop could have never envisioned the incredible possibilities for his pneumatic tyre. Unfortunately Dunlop did not stay with the company long enough to share in his inventions unforeseen global success. In 1896 at the age of fifty-six, he sold the company name and transferred all associated patents to his partner William DuCros for three thousand pounds. Dunlop was given a modest severance of one thousand, five hundred shares and retired to Dublin to live out his days.

John Boyd Dunlop died on 23 October 1921 in Dublin, Ireland at the age of eighty-one years old. Though Robert William Thomson was the first to invent and patent the pneumatic tyre in 1845, it took forty-five years for time to finally catch up to its technology. This is why the name John Boyd Dunlop will forever be synonymous with this great invention of comfort and mobility.

Timing is Everything.

"Courtesy of Brian Elsey and www.historyworld.co.uk."

Kirkpatrick Macmillan.

"Courtesy of Dumfries Museum."

## Kirkpatrick Macmillan

Born 2 September 1812 in Keir, Dumfries and Galloway, Scotland.
Died 26 January 1878 in Keir, Dumfries and Galloway, Scotland.

Credited with inventing the rear-wheel pedal-driven bicycle.

Since the dawn of time man has wanted to stretch the boundaries of nature, to go faster, to go further and to test the limits of ones imagination. As Aldous Huxley once said, "Speed provides the one great modern pleasure." The bicycle gave man a way to experience the great outdoors once only realized in ones imagination. The concept of the bicycle was first introduced to the world with the sketches of Gian Giacomo Caprotti, a pupil of Leonardo De Vinci in 1493. Unfortunately Giacomo's concepts never materialized into a useable prototype. Nearly three hundred fifty years would pass before the world could experience its first bicycle ride. Throughout the years that followed many variations of the Velocipedes would appear. A Velocipede is defined as any human-powered vehicle with one or more wheel. The most popular genre of Velocipedes is the bicycle with front-wheel pedals. By the late 19th century the bicycle was the fastest and the most eco-friendly mode of transportation on the entire earth. Kirkpatrick Macmillan was the first person to ever build a bicycle that had its primary mechanical components located on it rear wheel.

Most of the evidence substantiating Macmillan's claim as the first person to invent a rear-wheel pedal-driven bicycle derives from the research of his nephew James Johnson during the 1890's. Johnson claimed that his uncle, a blacksmith by trade, invented the first rear-wheel pedal-driven bicycle in 1839. Unfortunately none of his affirmations could ever be substantiated. Some historians have even suggested that many of the claims were simply fabrications orchestrated by Johnson. Though Johnson never was able to present any concrete evidence to support his uncle's claim, he always said he possessed the validating evidence. One piece of evidence Johnson was able to present was that his uncle was the first person ever to receive a moving vehicle violation in recorded history. The event occurred in the evening of 6 June 1842. As recorded in The Glasgow Argus on 9 June 1842. Macmillan's plan was to give his contraption a good testing by pedaling to his sister's home in Glasgow, then to return home. The entire journey was approximately one hundred forty miles round-trip. The first night of his journey he stayed over in Old Comnock for a much needed rest. The following morning he proceeded to Glasgow. Along the way on the outskirts of Glasgow in Gorbals, he decided to venture on to the pedestrian pavement. Soon after an intrigued crowd began to convey around Kirkpatrick and his velocipede, within the commotion a child was struck inadvertently by the bicycle and fell to the ground. Fortunately, the child did not sustain any injuries as reported by the press. Subsequently, the Gorbals' South Side Police were summoned and issued Macmillan a five shilling fine.

38

The following day when Macmillan appeared in court, the judge offered to pay his fine in exchange for a ride on Macmillan's contraption. There are two plaques posted at the Courthill Smithy where affectingly referred to by his fellow townspeople, "Daft Pate", once built his velocipede. The plaque that commemorates the one hundredth anniversary of his invention very accurately illustrates his accomplishments with a quote from the poem, *The Problem* by Ralph Waldo Emerson, "He builted better than he knew."

As Macmillan's bicycle gained popularity, counter-claims attempting to stake claim as the true creator of this modern marvel soon began to emerge. The most prominent of these counter-claims derived from Thomas McCall. McCall was born in Penpont, Scotland in 1834 and died in Kilmarnock 1904. McCall attested he created the first bicycle in 1869. James Johnson claimed McCall's designs were merely composites of Macmillan's previous designs. It can never be proven without a reasonable doubt who was the True inventor of the rear-wheel pedal-driven bicycle. But what can be substantiated is that McCall is responsible for improvements upon Macmillan's invention by introducing a breaking apparatus for the bicycle. He was also the first person to commercially sell bicycles out of his workshop in Kilmarnock.

Whether it was Macmillan or McCall whom truly invented the bicycle first, whomever it was he was undoubtedly Scottish.

Sir Robert Watson-Watt.
 "Courtesy of The Watson-Watt Society of Brechin and www.watsonwatt.org."

## Sir Robert Watson-Watt

A Physicist and inventor.

He is credited with inventing the R.A.D.A.R., Radio Detection and Ranging.

The invisible weapon that changed the tides of

World War II.

                    Robert Watson-Watt was born on 5 Union Street, Brechin, Angus, Scotland, on Wednesday 13 April 1892. As a child this son of a carpenter, attended the Damacre Primary School. While at Damacre, young Robert took an early interest in science. Due to his scholastic efforts he was awarded a scholarship to Brechin High School as well as University College, Dundee. At the time he attended University, Dundee was part of St. Andrews University. At University, academic excellence continued for Watson-Watt. Gradually acquiring an acute aptitude for the sciences, in 1910 he won the Carnelley Prize for chemistry and a class medal for Ordinary Natural Philosophy. In 1912, he graduated with a bachelor degree in Electrical Engineering. His first paid job after receiving his bachelor degree was as the assistant to the Chair of Physics at University College Dundee, Professor William Peddle.

                    When the First World War erupted Watson-Watt wanted to be involved in the British efforts towards victory. In 1915, he joined the Meteorology Department at the Royal Aircraft Factory in Farnborough, England. As a member of the Meteorology Department his post assignment was to investigate the effects of radio ionized signals in order to warn pilots of looming thunderstorms.

The methodology he applied to acquire his findings was by detecting and recording the ionized radio signals when they hit the surface of the earth. During World War I Germany directed Zeppelins in a barrage of attacks on Royal Air Force bases and surrounding towns around Britain. Regrettably, the only defense Great Britain possessed at the time was anti-aircraft machine guns that discouragingly did not reach the altitude at which the Zeppelins flew. In early June 1917, the German threat intensified when aerial attacks by fourteen Gotha Bombers descended upon English towns. With each bomber carrying one ton of explosions, nearly one-thousand civilians were either killed or wounded during what was later known as the deadliest air raid of the war. After these subsequent attacks the Royal military authorities were convinced an early warning system was critical to defend their Kingdom.

Meanwhile, Watson-Watt was gaining critical knowledge and experience he would later use in the coming years. In 1924, he moved to Ditton Park near Slough in Berkshire, England. While living in Ditton Park, he was employed by the Wireless Station of the Air Ministry Meteorological Office in Aldershot, England. In 1927, he became employed at the Radio Research Station, after they merged with the National Physics Laboratories (NPL). In 1933, he was appointed the Superintendent of the new Radio Department in Teddington, England. In 1934, Great Britain faced a precarious war-time predicament never faced on the Isle throughout its prolonged history. With Germany's dramatic buildup of armaments unseen since the end of the First World

War and Hitler's appointment as supreme chancellor, the prospect of another World War became eminent. The greatest risk Great Britain faced was looming threats of a Nazi air-raid on civilians. The cause for their preeminent concern derived from the fact Germany's airfields were only approximately a twenty minute flight to England. As a result, Nazi Luftwaffe bombers could drop their payloads and return safely back to their airbases in Germany prior to British fighter planes ever being able to reach altitudes where they could retaliate. In addition, British anti-aircraft weaponry could not shot down the bombing planes at the altitudes the Luftwaffe were flying. The only feasible solution the British Air Force could ascertain was a constant rotation of fighter planes in the air at all times. Unfortunately this idea was impractical due to its inherent expense of manpower and fighter planes. Another, more practical solution was desperately in need. The following year the British Air Ministry launched a committee headed by Sir Henry Tizard to advance the air defense around the British Isle. Their first attempt at an early warning defense system was carried out with the use of sound detection, but resulted with only limited success. Early that same year Watson-Watt was summoned to meet with the Director of Scientific Research at the Air Ministry; H.E. Wimperis. Initially the Air Ministry requested Watson-Watt to examine the possibilities of creating a death-ray with the use of radiation to defend against a German aerial assault. Though Watson-Watt felt the idea was more science fiction than science he hastily took the assignment.

Quickly Watson-Watt returned with calculations that his assistant, Arnold Wilkins computed to rebuke the death-ray premise. He proposed rather than to try to pursue a means of defense through destruction, it might be more fruitful to pursue the possibilities of the use of radio waves as a defense against Nazi air attacks.

On 26 February 1935, Watson-Watt and his assistant performed the first successful experiment employing radar detection to locate a flying aircraft. The fundamental objective behind his radar was to detect the distance, direction and the bearing of approaching enemy aircraft. Due to the eminent danger of approaching Nazi bombers, Watson-Watt and his team did not manufacture any new mechanical components for this initial experiment. Rather choosing to utilize readily available existing materials. The demonstration took place under the watchful eyes of Hugh Dowding, Commander of the Royal Air Force Fighter Command and Watson-Watt, on a field in Daventry, England. The transmitter of the radio waves was emitted out of the BBC shortwave station 10 Kilometers away. The receiver of the radio waves was located inside a Morris Bakery delivery truck on a field in Stowe Nine Church nearby. At 9:45 am a Hayward bomber made its first pass over the designated area. Unfortunately this first pass did not produce any results. Then the bomber made another pass over the predetermined site. The radio signal was bounced off the bomber flying above. This time echoes of very good amplitude came across the detection screen. The radar signal subsequently allowed the ground crew to see the aircraft and detect its approximate location. Despite its haste of preparation,

44

the experiment was a resounding success. The breakthrough was achieved! With the success of this initial display, a full-scale demonstration was the next step. Chain Home was the name given to this early warning radar system. Its operational capacities allowed it to detect aircraft at heights of twenty thousand feet. Though initially there were some kinks that needed to be ironed out before it could be considered fully operational. Soon after the corrections were carried out, additional towers were built stretching across the entire eastern and southern borders of Great Britain. At the commencement of the Battle of Britain nineteen towers were fully operational. By the conclusion of the Second World War fifty towers stretched across the coast.

The completion and integration of the world's first air defense system did not arrive a moment too soon. After France fell to the Nazi's, Great Britain became Hitler's next focus of attention. Referred to as Operation Sea Lion by the Nazi's, Germany planned to win control of the English Channel and then the British Isle. The Nazi's began to bomb airfields and radar towers around southern England from July to September of 1940. On 7 September 1940, the Nazi Luftwaffe Bombers turned their attention onto the City of London and so the Blitz began. The Royal Air Force was outnumbered four-to-one to their Nazi counterparts. But with the endowment of Watson-Watt's Radar Detection System, the RAF was able to focus their strengths strategically onto a small number of enemy targets for optimal results, therefore greatly increasing the possibilities of success. The RAF paid a heavy cost for victory in the Battle of Britain.

But without the Radar Detection technology they had in their possession, British causalities would have been significantly magnified.

The radar and the technological advancements that followed truly resurfaced the face of the earth. Radars are now standard equipment on every airplane manufactured. They assist air traffic controllers keeping passengers on nearly one hundred thousand daily commercial flights safe. To the effect that flying on a commercial airline is sixty-five times safer than driving an automobile.

They are also used by police offers to detect speeding cars. As the story goes, while living in Canada Watson-Watt was pulled over for speeding. He then told the police officer something to the effect that if he knew all those years ago that his invention would be used on himself, he would have possibly refrained from inventing it.

For recognition of his contributions to the war effort Watson-Watt was bestowed the honour of knighthood by the Royal Crown in 1942, Order of the Bath. In addition he was also appointed a Fellow of the Royal Society in 1941 and a Fellow of the Royal Aeronautical Society. In 1958, he wrote a book titled: *Three Steps to Victory*, chronicling his accounts of how he developed the RADAR. After living through one of the most preeminent periods in the world's history, Sir Robert Watson-Watt passed away on Wednesday 5 December 1973 at the age of eighty-one in the picturesque city of Inverness. He is buried with his third wife in the churchyard of Holy Trinity Episcopal Churchyard in Pitlochry, Scotland. His name might be forgotten by some, but his efforts never will.

Home Chain Radio transmitter towers
"Courtesy of The Watson-Watt Society of Brechin and www.watsonwatt.org."

James Goodfellow.

"Courtesy of James Goodfellow."

## Sir James Goodfellow

Born in Paisley, Renfrewshire, Scotland, 1937.

Invented and Patented the Personal Identification Number (PIN) and the
Automatic Teller Machine (ATM) technology in 1965.
It was originally and practically called the Automatic Cash Dispenser.

There are over two million cash machines in use
throughout the world today. To say it modestly the ATM and PIN have
revolutionized the landscape of everyday banking more than any other
creation of modern times. After the Second World War the banking
industry under pressure from trade unions throughout the United
Kingdom desired to close their branches early on Saturday mornings.
This would enable the wage earners of these particular branches leisure
time to shop and spend their pay checks. Furthermore, this concept
would save the branches from paying these workers for a full Saturday
wage. Additionally, the banks wanted to continue providing their
services to the public. At this intersection technology and James
Goodfellow crossed paths.

At this time James Goodfellow was employed as a
Development Engineer by Kelvin Hughes, part of Smiths Industries. As a
member of the staff whom possessed prior experience in the design of
both digital and dispensing systems James was assigned by Tony Davies,
General Manager, and Geoffrey Constable, Chief Engineer, the
responsibility of figuring out a way for the account holders of a particular

49

branch the ability to obtain access to their money while the bank was closed. The quandary Goodfellow faced was how to create a secure, consumer friendly, practical mechanism that would allow customers the ability to access their money during non-business working hours of the branch. If the task was not daunting enough it all had to be accomplished within the technical limitations of 1965. It must be noted this was a time unlike today banks were not on-line and electrical record-keeping did not exist at the magnitude it operates today. After several weeks he emerged with the concept for what would eventually become the premise behind Patent GB # 1,197,183 issued on 2 May 1966 and the subsequent U.S. Patent # 3,905,461, plus 13 other significant countries. Each branch customer would be issued a coded token, i.e. the bank card. In addition a second piece of customer sensitive security was also added. This was an individual sequence of four-digit numbers that would be inputted into the machine to access the cash. "From each individual coded token, the system derived an effective unique PAN, Personal Access Number, which now could only respond to an effective unique PIN, Personal Identification Number." Goodfellow's Personal Papers. If the customer entered the correct PIN corresponding to the correct PAN, the machine would dispense the allotted amount of cash. While if the user attempted three unsuccessful entries of the PIN code, the user would be blocked from ATM usage. The unassigned user had a one in ten thousand chance of guessing the unknown PIN correctly. The PIN entering process was very advantageous for the banks to incorporate due to its multiple combinations of code possibilities.

In addition, this system had low start-up and instillation costs in addition to being a very reliable two part security system. The keypad configuration of numbers Goodfellow decided upon has also become the universal standard on every mobile phone and television remote control produced world-wide, with numbers being arranged in three columns of three with the zero right under the eight.

It should be noted at the time of Goodfellow's invention of the PIN and Automated Cash Dispenser there were several alternative approaches he had the opportunity of incorporating into his endeavour. Several examples of such potential alternatives were, radioactive doping, magnetic signals, imbedding a gold strip onto the bank card, the use of figure prints, retinal pattern scanning and the use of a voice recognition device. Though they were all feasible alternatives, none were practical. Several of the reasons why they were not chosen by Goodfellow are as followed, they were not secure enough, their potential negative public perception, they were not easy to mass produce and in the end they were not cost effective.

You may think the man whom invented possibly the most important technology of the twentieth century would be swimming in money. Regrettably the way the laws were written in the UK at the time of his invention as a Research and Development Engineer employed by Kelvin Hughes, which was part of Smith Industries, the ownership of the patents and all subsequent potential revenue streams that would materialize from such patents belonged to the employer and not to the true inventor of the technology, James Goodfellow.

51

However the laws regarding such intellectual ownership and the potential for future financial gains from such ownership changed in 1977, though unfortunately the law did not allow for Goodfellow's inventions to be retroactively included. The only financial payment Goodfellow was allowed to receive was $1 US for every signature on a patent application. In total fifteen applications were made to major countries throughout the world, giving him $15 US or about £10 sterling. Unfortunately that was all he was allowed to receive at the time of his invention due to how the laws were written. To this day, he does not receive any residual royalties, not a single cent for his invention, but what he does have is the satisfaction of knowing he invented a machine that altered the banking landscape forever.

Almost immediately after his patents were issued counter claims of the True Creator of the PIN and Automatic Cash Dispenser soon began to appear. As early as 1967, unsubstantiated claims supporting no evidence and no patent record began to emerge. One such claim that emerged was from another Scotsman named John Shepherd-Barron. Shepherd-Barron was born on 23 June 1925 in Shillong, India and died on 15 May 2010 in Inverness, Scotland. He was also named an Officer of the Order of the British Empire. Though his design for an ATM machine was the first to be installed into a bank in 1967, it is Goodfellow's 1966 patented technology that is still popularly in use today. Shepherd-Barron was assigned by De La Rue instruments to create an automatic cash dispenser to dole out cash to bank patrons twenty four hours a day. The first devise he installed was the Barclay Bank branch in Enfield, North London. This first machine was called the DACS, De La Rue Automatic Cash System. His security system was slightly different from the one Goodfellow used, the magnetic strip card and a PIN. Shepherd-Barron's security system consisted of a card that was imbedded with a small amount of radioactive carbon-14 that would match up with a six to four digit PIN code.

In acknowledgement for his contributions as the, "Patentor of the Personal Identification Number and for services to the banking Industry", James Goodfellow was awarded an Officer of the Order of the British Empire by Queen Elizabeth II in 2006.

In addition, among the other Engineers employed at the Laboratory the Automated Cash Dispenser Goodfellow was involved with was affectingly referred to as Jim's money machine.

Other than the additional functions the present day ATM can perform, account transfers, balance inquiries, deposits in addition to withdraws, the PIN and Automated Cash Dispenser Patented in 1966, virtually has remained unchanged for the past forty plus years.

Adam Smith.

## Adam Smith

Founder of free market economics, a Scottish moral philosopher and pioneer of political economics.

Adam Smith was born on 5 June 1723 in Kirkcaldy, Fife, Scotland. Since a confirmation of the precise date of his birth is impossible to make, the date documented on his baptismal records is the date widely recognized. His father's name was also Adam Smith. Regrettably he passed away before young Adam was born. His mother's name was Margaret Douglas. Smith lived with his mother in their family home on 220 High Street until her death. As a child young Adam attended elementary school at the Burgh School of Kirkcaldy. Presently it is called the Kirkcaldy High School. While at Burgh his days were filled with an engaging curriculum of mathematics, history, Latin and writing. In 1737, at the age of fourteen he entered Glasgow University. After graduating in 1740 with the Snell Exhibition Scholarship, he soon traveled to Oxford England to attend the renowned Balliol College. Smith studied intensely at Balliol until 1746 when he left prior to the completion of his scholarship. It is said he was rather dismissive towards the master of the college. It is suggested Smith regarded the professors at Glasgow University at a far superior level compared to Oxfords masters. To say the least, he did not have an enjoyable experience during his time at Oxford. His opinion was on the vine that the great minds of the time were not attached to the profession of teaching, due to the fact they could earn far more wealth in other occupations.

In 1748, after leaving Oxford with the sponsorship of Lord Henry
Kames and connections obtained by his mother's family, Smith began
his series of public lectures on moral philosophy, ethics, law and political
economic at the University of Edinburgh. The discipline of moral
philosophy is presently studied under the umbrella of Social Sciences. In
1751, he was appointed professor of Logic at Glasgow University. The
following year he transferred his professorship to the subject of moral
philosophy. This in turn would become his life's work. This period in the
world would later be referred to as the Scottish Enlightenment. During
his time lecturing at the University of Edinburgh Smith resided at
Panmure House from 1788 until 1790. The Edinburgh Business School
at Heriot-Watt University purchased and restored the premises in 2008.

Smith published his first book in 1759, titled:
*The Theory of Moral Sentiment.* In his book Smith wanted to explain the
source of mankind's ability to form moral judgments. One of the
preeminent themes encompassing his writings was the theory that all
human actions inadvertently should aspire to create unintended
consequences beneficial for all parties involved. He considered this the
uncontrollable variable in all human actions. Within his book he
emphasized the premise that it was human nature to aspire to be loved
and to be lovely and those humans craved to achieve this merit through
the appreciation of others. In 1776, after nine years of extensive research,
Smith released the world's preeminent document on economics ever
written.

It was titled: *An Inquiry into the Natural Causes of the Wealth of Nations.* It was enormously influential from the moment it was published. His work is considered by many throughout the world as the precursor to the modern discipline of economics. At the time Smith penned his book the most popular strategy nations used to quantify their wealth was to measure their accumulated stock-pile of precious medals such as gold and silver. Subsequently, import goods were heavily taxed, therefore artificially allowing domestic industries the liberty to flourish. Even if the similar imported good was of superior quality. To promote this artificial domestic superiority of goods a vast network was established to stifle any foreign competition. Throughout Europe protectionism laws were implemented to fend off foreign economic expansion. Several examples of restrictions imposed by European countries were as followed, subsidies given to exporters, petitions to the King to stifle domestic competition and placing embargos on all intellectual ideas. Smith disagreed with this premises whole heartily. He implored a nation's true wealth did not derive from its hording of precious medals but rather from what the country produced and what gave the people of the country that produced these products true happiness. Today this is called a nations gross national product. He favored a free enterprise form of economy where the quality of goods would be balanced by competitive pricing rather than embargos of imports. Thus, the promoting of a superior quality product at a competitive price matched with the demands from the market.

He referred to this hand's off, laissez-faire economy as a system of perfect liberty. As an advocate against big business and big government, Smith supported the sentiment if nations and therefore the people within these nations were left alone to decide and maneuver within their own designed economic world, they would be better off than within an economic system controlled by a government of any capacity. He felt ones self-interest indirectly would positively benefits society and the people within the society. Therefore with free market policies in place that promoted fairness of free trade, societies would be without the need for economic control of a monarch. He referred to this as the invisible hand theory. In a free market society the producer and the consumer would benefit positively. He also felt the allowance of foreign born influence regarding to innovation of production was a powerful generator of trade and wealth. He also felt for a society to be considered successful the basic necessities of life must be given to all its inhibitors without regard to their social or economic status. Each inhibitor of the society must have the right to adequate food, clothing and lodging if nothing else. He also believed by donating your time or goods to the underprivileged gives a two-fold reward. Smith illustrated in his perfect economy there was also no room for special privilege group. *The Wealth of Nations* also wheeled its guidance and influence on the political ambitions of several of the founding fathers of the United States. Thomas Jefferson and James Madison attributed Smith's influential hand during debates regarding the creation of a National Bank and formulation of militias or a standard army during the early stages of the formation of the

United States. In addition to their shared sentiment that all people deserve the right to pursue ones own liberty, prosperity and happiness. His influence was also felt during the writing of the United Stated Constitution in 1787-88. Smith's influence was also acknowledged by the British Prime Minister William Pitt.

A decade after writing *The Wealth of Nations,* Smith worked as a comptroller of customs in Kirkcaldy. In 1787, he was appointed rector of Glasgow University.

Adam Smith died in Edinburgh on Saturday 17 July 1790 at sixty-seven years of age. He was laid to rest in the churchyard at Canongate.

Post mortem commensurations:

His face was portrayed on the £50 note issued by the Clydesdale Bank of Scotland in 1981 and the £20 note issued by the Bank of England. This marked the first time a Scotsman was featured on an English note.

There is also a statue of Smith on the Royal Mile in Edinburgh outside St. Giles Cathedral.

Smith possessed an acute wisdom on how human societies actually operated. In the two-hundred plus years since his death he is still considered the preeminent voice of economic thought. The *Wealth of Nations* also set a tone for all future social science studies. With a combination of empirical work as well as his observations in conjunction with logic and philosophy, Smith formed economic theories that are still relevant today.

Sir Sandford Fleming. "Courtesy of Fleming College, Canada."

## Sir Sandford Fleming

Distinguished engineer and creator of the concept of Standard Time.

Sir Sandford Fleming was born on Sunday 7 January 1827, in Kirkcaldy, Fife, Scotland, to parents Elizabeth and Andrew Fleming. On 24 April 1845, eighteen year old Sanford and his older brother David left the sea port of Glasgow on a ship named *The Brilliant* and traveled across the Atlantic Ocean to carve out a new life for each other in Canada. The brothers Fleming first landed in what was then referred to as Canada West, presently its called Ontario. Eventually after a few years of bouncing from town to town in the western part of the country the new immigrants settled in Peterborough, Ontario where the friendly faces of several cousins resided in 1847. With the training and experience he possessed from his days as a young man in Scotland, Sandford soon gained employment with several railway companies throughout Canada. While employed with the Intercolonial Railroad in 1863, Fleming and a team of surveyors laid out the plans that would eventually connect New Brunswick and Nova Scotia with the rest of Canada. He was also a member of the team employed by the Canada Pacific Railway responsible for the first survey of a railroad route that would connect the entire country. In time he was promoted to engineer by several railways throughout the country. In 1867, he was appointed Engineer in Chief of the largest Canadian public works project of the nineteenth century, the Intercolonial Railway.

As defined in the New Webster's Comprehensive Dictionary of the English Language, Standard Time is the time in a country or locality, usually established by legislation or local custom, expressed in relation to a selected meridian. Prior to the concept of Standard Time, it was accepted practice that most major cities throughout the world would keep their own time by utilizing some sort of solar timekeeping device maintained by a popular centered clock in town. The challenge behind this method of timekeeping is its universal accuracy. Since early in his career as a surveyor and engineer of railways, Fleming was an advocate of the adoption of a universal Standard Time. He witnessed first hand how inaccuracies in time could affect the arrival and departure service provided by a railway. During the nineteenth century in North America alone there were one hundred forty-four official time zones, making accuracy of arrival and departures virtually impossible. Fleming was convinced he had figured out a remedy for this worldly dilemma, he only needed an audience in which to entertain his idea. As one of the founders of the Royal Canadian Institute in Toronto in 1849, Fleming was allowed such a platform to express his revolutionary concept. At the Royal Canadian Institute Conference of 1879, Fleming first publically demonstrated his recommendations for a Universal Standard Time. He proposed a standard twenty-four hour clock for the entire world for reckoning time, by dividing the world into twenty-four time zones. He substantiated his suggestions with the use of the anti-meridian of Greenwich, now referred to as the International Date Line as the starting point for calculating time. He referred to this concept of time keeping as Cosmic Time.

Due to his insightful presentation at the conference, Standard Time was instituted by the railroad industries of the United States and Canada at noon on 18 November 1883. Fleming's next pursuit was to flex his political influence at the International Prime Meridian Conference in October 1884, in Washington D.C... The conference was held at the request of the President of the United States of America, Chester A. Arthur. It was attended by forty-one dignitaries from twenty-five countries. Spearheaded by Fleming, Abbe, and William Frederick Allen, the Secretary of the U.S. Railways, twenty-two countries voted on where the prime meridian should be located on the globe. The purpose for the prime meridian is to determine where 0° longitude would be located and then in accordance with the rotation of the earth determine Standard Time. The Prime Meridian 0° longitude and the International Date Line 180° longitude are imaginary lines that cut the world into half, separating the earth into the west and eastern hemispheres. The delegates voted for the International Prime Meridian to be centered at the Royal Observatory, Greenwich, England, hence referred to as the Greenwich Meridian. To a great majority of people walking the earth today the measure of establishing a way to calculate a Universal Standard Time largely is taken for granted. But the concept of an International Standard Time and the dividing of the globe into twenty-four time zones could be considered one of the greatest innovations of the Victorian Age.

The father of Standard Time was also involved in other innovations throughout his lifetime. He designed Canada's first postal stamp in 1851, referred to as the Three-penny Beaver. The beaver is the national animal of Canada.

He also designed an early form of in-line skate. He also served in the military with the 10th Battalion Volunteer Rifles of Canada. Presently they are called the Royal Regiment of Canada. He was appointed to the rank of Captain on 1 January 1862 and retired from active duty in 1865. Later in his life he donated his summer home and its ninety-five acre property to the city of Halifax, later to be renamed Dingle Park. In 1897, he was knighted by Queen Victoria, the Most Distinguished Order of Saint Michael and Saint George.

Standard Time based on time zones was put into law in the United States on 19 March 1918. The law was titled the Standard Time Act. Though it was not until 1929, when acceptance of the concept of universal time zones and Standard Time became worldwide.

Sir Sandford Fleming died on Thursday 22 July 1915, at the age of eighty-eight in Halifax, Nova Scotia. He is buried in Canada's National Cemetery, Beechwood in Ottawa, Ontario.

The name Sandford Fleming and his influence on the human condition, is immortalized in the town of Fleming, Saskatchewan, named after him in 1882, Fleming Hall at Queen's University in Kingston, Ontario, named after him in 1901, and in Fleming College, Ontario, named after him in 1967.

Mr JAMES WATT.

James Watt.

## James Watt

He was a Mathematical Instrument Maker, Entrepreneur, and Inventor whom
improved upon the design of the Steam Engine in which ignited the Industrial
Revolution.
He is considered one of the most influential people in all human history.


Though he did not invent the Steam Engine,
he is responsible for enhancing its productive capabilities. Watt's
modifications on the Steam Engine became the flint that ignited the
Industrial Revolution and thus the modern world.
James Watt was born on Thursday 19 January 1736, in Greenock,
Renfrewshire, Scotland. He was born into a family that placed great
emphasis on religious piety and higher education. These values were not
just the virtues of his parents, but ethics well established within his
lineage. His fraternal grandfather, Thomas Watt was a mathematics
instructor and Baillie to the Baron of Cartsburn. His mother's name was
Agnes Muirhead. James was named after his father, James Watt Sr.
Throughout his life his father was engaged in numerous occupations. For
a time he held positions of treasurer and magistrate of Greenock. He was
also a ship chandler, a shipwright, and repairer of nautical instruments.
Due to his incessant poor health young James was hindered from
attending school regularly. On those rare occasions when he had the
strength he attended the Greenock Grammar School. During those brief
moments in the classroom he excelled in mathematics, in particular
geometry.
He was also an avid reader.

After his mother passed away when he was eighteen years of age, he ventured to Glasgow to take on an apprenticeship in mathematical instrument making. Heeding to the advisement of one of his fellow confidants and professor at the University of Glasgow, Dr. Robert Dick, James moved to London in June 1755 to continue his apprenticeship. After some time in London he returned to Glasgow with the anticipation of opening an instrument making shop of his own. Regrettably his apprenticeship training did not fulfill the prerequisite requirements of the Glasgow Guild of Hammermen. Therefore unfortunately he was forbidden from opening his own mechanical repair shop. Until the hands of fate eased young James into an auspicious opportunity he inadvertently was preparing for all his life. The University of Glasgow was reloading their MacFarlane Observatory. In 1757, with a stroke of good fortune he was offered the opportunity to open a repair business on the University grounds.

Prior to the development of the Steam Engine, man was solely dependant on the power of his own muscle. Then he developed the ability to harness the elements with the creation of the water mill, though its capacities limited its productivity. Then in 1698, Thomas Savery produced the first Steam Engine. Its simple function was to convert the heat energy of the steam into useable mechanical energy. The Steam Engine was the first machine that had the ability to produce energy that was not hampered by topographical limitations such as a water supply, wind or space to draft animals. In 1712, a blacksmith named Thomas Newcomen made several alterations to Savery's engine. Due to its practicality, this engine was phased into popular use during the 1720's. Soon the Newcomen Steam Engine effectively replaced water pump technology as the predominant mechanism for pumping water out of mines. Then time, fate and a man named James Watt collided at the cusp of the Industrial Revolution.

The catalyst that propelled James Watt into immortality arrived one day in 1763. Toiling away at his workbench he was presented with a Newcomen atmospheric Steam Engine to repair for the University. Though he was able to successfully repair the engine, he discovered it was grossly inefficient due to several design flaws. Through his investigations he realized three-forth of the heat that radiating from the steam was wasted during every cycle, thus requiring larger amounts of coal to produce optimal results. He felt given some time he could refine the engine and make it more efficient. Watt needed to figure out a way to keep the cylinder containing the steam hot at all times. He soon discovered if he built another alternate, separate cylinder called a condenser his problem would be solved. The condenser would cool the steam, thus the amount of energy produced would increase with greater efficiency and at a more consistent pace.

On 5 January 1769, he received a patent for his innovation to the Steam Engine. Though unfortunately due to his financial constraints, there was a delay of ten years in the development of a working model for his new and improved Steam Engine. During this ten year hiatus Watt was forced to take up alternate means of employment. During this period he teamed up with John Wilkinson.

He was the man that developed the first precision boring techniques utilized in cannon making. He also was employed as a surveyor and then as a civil engineer for eight years. He soon obtained the necessary financial stability he desperately needed to produce his Steam Engine from Professor Joseph Black of the University of Glasgow and more significantly from John Roebuck, founder of the Carron Works. As gratitude for his financial contributions, Roebuck was granted a two-thirds ownership of all Watt's patents, though regrettably within a four years time Roebuck had succumbed to bankruptcy. He subsequently sold his holdings to Matthew Boulton in 1774. Boulton an entrepreneur at heart could foresee the tremendous projected potential of Watt's Steam Engine and intended on profiting from it. At first the working arrangement established by Boulton and Watt was one of employer and employee. Though gradually it transformed into a partnership that would continue for the next twenty-five year until Watt's patents expired in 1800.By 1776, the first engines were beginning to be manufactured at Boulton's Soho Engineering Works near Birmingham, England. These first engines were predominantly built for mines around Cornwall. Though the engines were not built by Boulton & Watt, the dual would serve as consultant engineers supervising their assembly. Shrewd businessmen from the beginning, Boulton & Watt undercut their competition by only charging one-third the cost of coal that would be used by the Newcomen engine.

During the next six years Watt focused his creative attentions on refinements towards his Steam Engine. In the pursuit to broaden the accessibility of his engine Watt's first modification was to provide the pistons of the engine the ability of reciprocating motion. Industries involved in grinding, weaving, milling as well as distilleries, greatly benefited by these alterations. A crank operated mechanism would have worked best, but was earlier patented by James Pickard in 1780. The following year Watt patented his adaptation of a similar premise called the Sun and Planet gear. This patent was accepted on 25 October 1781 and enrolled on 23 February 1782. Other modifications he rendered unto his engine were the Double-acting and Compound engines, patented accepted on 14 March 1782 and enrolled on 4 July 1782. Refinements continued at a rapid pace with the Steam Indicator and the Throttle Valve. The Throttle Valve allowed its user the ability to regulate the speed and power of the engine. Of all the innovations Watt fostered in his lifetime his creation of the Parallel Motion Link he patented in 1784 was his proudest achievement. Its ability to produce straight line motion established the Parallel Motion Link as the essential component of the double acting engine and the predecessor to rotary motion. He also patented the Centrifugal Governor in 1788, which automatically controlled the speed of the engine in addition to being a pressure gauge for the cylinder. All of Watt's patented improvements enabled his engine to become five times more efficient in fuel and output compared to the Newcomen Engine.

James Watt also contributed to the modernization of the copying industry. On 31 May 1780, he patented the Letter Copying

Press. This machine allowed its operator the ability to copy single letters, plans, drawings or any other document automatically by producing a reverse image of the original document. This apparatus was the predecessor to the modern-day scanner, laser printer and photocopier. A very easy to operate yet sophisticated apparatus it was used throughout the industrial world. Watt also contributed to the greater good of society with his contributions as a Civil Engineer planning the construction of canals, roads, railways and docks.

James Watt was bestowed numerous honoraries throughout his lifetime. He was appointed a Fellow of the Royal Society of London as well as Edinburgh, 1784. He was a member of the Lunar Society centered in Birmingham. This was a group of like minded scientists, artists and great thinkers. In 1787, he was elected a member of the Batavian Society for Experimental Philosophy of Rotterdam. In 1789, he was elected to the Society of Civil Engineers. In 1806, he was presented an honorary Doctor of Law from the University of Glasgow. In 1814, he was elected as a Foreign Member of the Academic des Sciences, Paris. His name is also forever immortalized in our modern-day lexicon. He credited with creating the term horsepower to describe a unit of power produced. In addition to the word Watt is used to a measure a unit of electrical, mechanical or thermal power equal to one joule.

After a distinguished life James Watt passed away at his country home in Handsworth, Birmingham on Wednesday 25 August 1819, at the age of eighty-three. He was buried on 2 September next to his long-time business partner Matthew Boulton and William Murdoch on the parish grounds of St. Mary's Church in Handsworth. After his death several statuaries of his likeness were erected throughout Scotland and England. One was placed near the vicinity of his birth and the Town Hall in Greenock. Another was placed at George Square in Glasgow, another on Prince Street in Edinburgh, another on the Riccarton campus grounds, Heriot-Watt University, Edinburgh, while another statue was placed on Broad Street in Birmingham, commemorating The Three Wise Men, Boulton, Murdoch and Watt. There is another in Chamberlain Square outside the Birmingham Central Library. There is also a statue in Piccadilly Gardens in Manchester, at the City Square in Leeds, and in Oxford University Museum of Natural History, as well as in Westminster Abby, which was later moved to St. Paul's Cathedral. He is also immortalized with a bust of his likeness at the Hall of Heroes at the William Wallace Monument at Stirling, along with the other fifteen greatest Scotsmen of All Time. In 2011, he was nominated to the inaugural call of inductees of the Scottish Engineering Hall of Fame.

There are also institutions of higher learning named after James Watt. The Watt Memorial Library with an Andrew Carnegie endowment in which was later absorbed into James Watt College founded in 1907, Greenock, the Heriot-Watt University,

Edinburgh and the University of Glasgow's Facility of Engineering headquarters called the James Watt Building. On May 2009, the Bank of England authorized his likeness along with his partner Matthew Boulton on the new £50 note. Finally, there are around fifty roads or streets named after him throughout the British Isle.

The English writer Aldous Huxley once so eloquently wrote of Watt's unmatched contributions in shaping the modern world with this quote, "To us, the moment 8:17 am means something-something very important, if it happens to be the starting time of our daily train. To our ancestors, such an odd eccentric instance was without significance-did not even exist. In inventing the locomotive, Watt and Stevenson were part inventors of time."

These symbols and more embody how James Watt, the catalyst to the Industrial Revolution will forever be remembered.

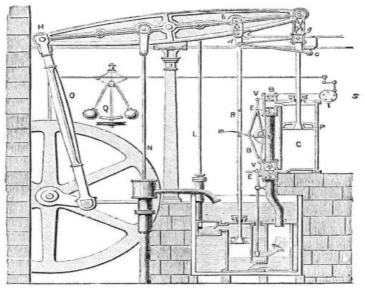

Watt's Steam Engine 1780, Popular Science Monthly Volume 12.
"Public Domain. Copyright has expired, life of the author plus 70 years in
United States, United Kingdom and Australia."

William Murdoch.

"Courtesy of the William Wallace National Monument- Hall of Heroes."
Personal Collection.

## William Murdoch

Best known for creating the technology behind the gas lantern as well as inventing the Oscillating stream engine.

Imagine living in a world before the gas light. Where as soon as the sun cleared the horizon darkness would capture the day and despair would rule throughout the land. Other than the risk of home invasion and theft of property or robbery, there was also the exorbitant amount of work and productivity that was lost when the sun set. With the invention of the gas lantern many of these earthly stresses were extinguished. The illumination of the interior quarters of residences and hamlets of commerce allowed the masses the ability to double the useable hours of the day.

William Murdoch was born on Wednesday 21 August 1754, at Bello Cottage in Lugar near Cumnock, East Ayrshire, Scotland, the second son of a millwright. The first twenty-three years of his life were spent in Lugar and Ayrshire. His intellectual endeavors began at the old Cumnock Kirk School. He attended the school until he was ten years of age. Soon after, young William attended the Auchinleck School where he excelled in Mathematics. For the next fifty-three years of his life, 1777 until 1830, he was employed by Boulton & Watt at the Soho Manufacturing facility near Birmingham in England. His primary responsibility while employed with Boulton & Watt was to manage the production of the steam engines being produced.

77

In 1779, he was transferred to their facilities in Cornwell, England. Due to his supreme work ethic and engineering mastery he was promoted to partner of the firm in 1810. He remained employed at that facility until he was seventy-six years of age.

In 1784, while employed with Boulton & Watt, Murdoch first created the Oscillating steam engine. The simple yet distinct difference behind Murdoch's engine construction and others of the time was that it did not require values to direct the steam in and out of its cylinders. That same year he was also involved with the technology behind Great Britain's first steam road locomotive, also referred to as a steam powered motor vehicle. As he flirted with steam road locomotion, he continued to pursue experiments on how to capture and contain gas from coal emissions. In the years prior to this modest man's invention, the most popular way to illuminate the interiors of quarters of ones home was with the use of oil and tallow burning lanterns. The major drawback behind using this method of lighting ones home was its high probability of house fires, inevitable loss of property and unforeseen death. A better, safer way of light interiors of homes was in desperate need. It is widely accepted Murdoch's gas lantern was invented around 1792. The ingenious technology behind his lantern was its ability to capture and store the gas released by the coal. His home on Cross Street in Redruth, England, was the first residence in the world to posses his gas lantern technology. With the successful venture of lighting his home completed, he soon launched a campaign to install his street lanterns throughout several city centers around England with resounding success. Creative uses for his gas lantern soon began to develop at a lighting pace. In the days prior to street lights, his gas lantern was the ideal aid for nightly returns home from visiting acquaintances or a brief stay at the local pub. The wayward traveler would carry the gas in a bladder tucked under his arm like a bagpipe with the gas traveling up a tube to the ignition in the lantern. Soon this concept was placed into permanent gas street lanterns. He never was able to capitalize financially from any of his inventions due to his lack of insight and realizing the importance in patenting his ideas. With the gas lantern being invented at the cusp of the Industrial Revolution, this single invention catapulted manufacturing levels to heights never before imagined. The extension of the work day allowed for greater levels of production and ultimately greater profits.

Several other note-worthy engineering feats and inventions of Murdoch were the steam-driven tricycle, a steam cannon, a worm-driven cylinder boring machine, underwater paint for ships, iron cement, a steam powered gun, and a D-slide valve. He also developed the world's first pneumatic tube messaging system. You may have seen this technology used at your local bank or supermarket. It is predominantly used to transfer excess amounts of cash from the register to a more secure location within the building.

After a well publicized life at the age of eighty-five years old the father of the Gas industry died at his home in Sycamore Hill, Penzance, England on Friday 15 November 1839. He was buried at St. Mary's Church in Handsworth, Birmingham, along with his two partners from the Soho Manufacturing facility, James Watt and Matthew Boulton. To acknowledge and commemorate Murdoch's technological achievements and contributions to the modern world, a bust of his likeness was included as one of the sixteen greatest men of Scotland at the Hall of Heroes at the William Wallace Monument in Stirling, Scotland. Furthermore, there is a statue on Broad Street, Birmingham, England titled the Three Wise Men. Also included with Murdoch are statutes of his partners Boulton and Watt.

Sidebar:

He replaced the H with a K in his surname when he moved to England, in order to relieve pronunciation problems by clients.

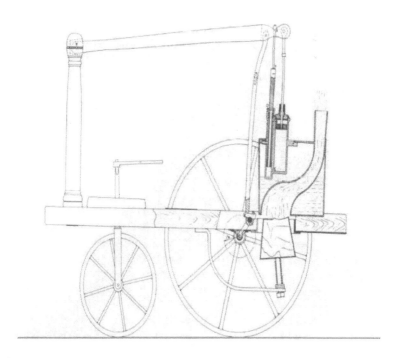

Murdoch Steam Carriage.

Sir Alexander Fleming.

"Courtesy of Wellcome Library, London."

## Sir Alexander Fleming

Discover of Penicillin. The world's first miracle drug and the most widely used antibiotic throughout the world.

Sir Alexander Fleming was born to Grace and Hugh Fleming on Saturday 6 August 1881 in a remote farm near Darvel, Lochfield, Ayrshire, Scotland. From an early age Alec as he was called at home, was intrigued with nature. Living his childhood with seven other siblings in rural Ayrshire, they never lacked opportunities to cultivate their imaginative minds. His father worked on an eight hundred acre farm, one mile from their home. When his father Hugh passed away, his older brother took on the responsibilities of tending to the farm and helped with the raising of the younger siblings. His other brother Thomas went to London after studying at Glasgow University to practice medicine. Young Alexander's formal education began at Loudoun Moor School and the Darvel School. He then attended the Kilmarnock Academy on a two-year scholarship. This was the first time in the life of twelve year old Alec which he spent time away from home. He stayed with his aunt during the week for school and then traveled home by train for the weekends. He then moved to London to join his brother Thomas, whom opened a medical practice where he was an Optometrist. After some time his elder sister and his other brother John soon followed to London. While he was in London he attended the Royal Polytechnic Institution, now called the University of Westminster. From

1900-1914, he was also a member of the Territorial Army serving with the London Scottish Regiment. This is similar to the Army Reserves in the United States. Soon after, his uncle left him a small inheritance of two hundred, fifty pounds. With this and a scholarship he earned in 1901 he then attended St. Mary's Hospital Medical School in London. He had a choice of three medical schools to attend all equidistant from his home. Not knowing anything regarding any particular institution he chose St. Mary's solely on the fact he previously played water polo against them. In 1908, as a student he earned the gold medal from the University of London, recognizing the top medical student at the institution.

Then the Great War broke out throughout Europe. During this tumultuous time he served as a captain with the Royal Army Medical Corp, concentrating his efforts in a makeshift lab studying battlefield wound infections as a bacteriologist. Through his inquiries he realized the antiseptics being applied on the battlefield only treated surface wounds and did not possess the ability to treat deeper wounds incurred by many of the soldiers. This unfortunately greatly diminished the body's ability to combat internal infections. Thus, more soldiers were dying from post-wound infections than their initial wounds. He suggested simply keeping the wounds dry and clean, but his suggestions were predominantly unheeded. After the Great War concluded he returned to London's St. Mary Hospital and intended on becoming a surgeon, but soon realized his interests would be best met within the discipline of bacteriology. In 1918, he became the assistant director of the Inoculation Department. This is where he first began to write scholastic papers on immunology. Immunology is a branch of biomedical science that focuses on all aspects of the immune system.

In 1928, he was named a professor of bacteriology and in 1948 he was named as an emeritus professor at the University of London.

Fleming had several other discoveries prior to his discovery of Penicillin. One such discovery was that Pus helped in the combat of Syphilis. He also discovered the enzymes in tears called Lysozyme had natural antibactcrial effects in 1923. Then the calendar turned to 3 September 1928. This date marked the day of his greatest discovery. After a month long holiday Fleming returned to his cluttered laboratory. He soon observed a mold was growing through a number of glass plates previously coated with Staphylococcus Aureus. He soon realized the Staph bacteria were killed off around thc mold in the contaminated dish. He would call this mold Penicillium Notatum or simply Penicillin. Penicillin became the world's first antibiotic or bacteria killer and revolutionized modern medicine. He then began to perform research tests on animals to prove his newly discovered Penicillin could kill other bacteria's and would not result in any side effects for the patient. Fleming published his findings in the British Journal of Experimental Pathology in 1929. In the ensuing years Penicillin would become the greatest medical breakthrough in history. Initially little interest was given to his findings. Not until the Second World War did Penicillin become used world wide for treating infections due to its ability to interfere with cell wall metabolism of bacteria. It is estimated that during World War II, 15% or around one-hundred fifty thousand injured Allied Force servicemen who were administered Penicillin was saved. The difference Penicillin offered battlefield medicine was that it not only treated the infections suffered by the soldiers it cured them. Soon Fleming began to shift his attention towards other medical inquiries. By the 1930's Penicillin's torch was picked up by two Oxford University scientists, Howard Florey and Ernst Chain. The three scientists would be awarded the Noble Peace Prize in 1945 in the category of Physiology or Medicine.

Fleming was also a member of the following academic societies throughout his lifetime:

- Fellow of the Royal Society of Edinburgh.
- Fellow of the Royal Society of London.
- Fellow of the Royal College of Surgeons of London.
- He was knighted in 1944 by King George VI.
- He was a member of the Pontifical Academy of Science and Honorary member of almost all the medical and scientific societies of the world.
- He was named Rector of Edinburgh University from 1951-1954.
- Named the President of the Society for General Microbiology.
- Awarded honorary doctorate degrees from nearly thirty European and American Universities and many others.

On Friday 11 March 1955 Sir Alexander Fleming died from a massive heart attack in London, England, at the age of seventy-three. He is buried at St. Paul's Cathedral.

Fleming often said, "I did not invent Penicillin. Nature did that. I only discovered it by accident." Birch pg.60.

"This signature is believed to be ineligible for copyright and therefore in the public domain because it falls below the required level of originality for copyright protection both in the United States and in the source country (if different). In this case, the source country (e.g. the country of nationality of the signatory) is believed to be Scotland."

Propranolol.

Cimetidine.

## Sir James Whyte Black

Sir James Black was a medical and pharmaceutical genius whom developed two of the world's greatest selling pharmaceutical drugs of all time: Propranolol, the first successful beta-blocker and Cimetidine, a remedy for stomach and peptic ulcer disease.

Sir James Black was born on Saturday 14 June 1924 in Uddingston, Lanarkshire, Scotland into a working class home. His father supported his family as a mining engineer and as a colliery manager. Due to the mobility of his father's occupation young James was brought up in Cowdenbeath, Fife. While living in Cowdenbeath he attended and graduated from Beath High School. While a student he always achieved high marks in mathematics though he never felt his aptitude was any sort of great gift. Thankfully his mathematics teacher named Mr. Waterson recognized his potentials and forced young James to take the prestigious St. Andrews University entrance exam. He achieved such high marks on the exam he was offered a scholarship to study at University at fifteen years of age. During his acceptance speech when he received his Nobel Prize, Dr. Black humbly credited his career successes to the academic rigor he received while studying at University. He recounted while attending St. Andrews he learned to substitute the indulgence of daydreaming with disciplined study. Following in his older brother's footsteps he earned his medical degree in 1946 from the University of St. Andrew. Soon after graduation and due to a lack of job prospects in the United Kingdom, he moved to Singapore for three years to lecture at the King Edward VII College of Medicine. This was an exciting time in the history of Scotland. In 1947, the National Health Service Act was passed. This program provides universal health care for the citizens of Scotland. During this period many of the countries medical universities were given great opportunities to expand. In 1950, Dr. Black returned to Great Britain. After some time without successfully landing employment he was offered a position at the University of Glasgow veterinary school. While there he focused his attentions on attempts to relieve an ailment called, Angina Pectoric. Angina Pectoric is the name given to the tightening pains in the chest that are caused by a lack of oxygen to the heart muscles. In many cases these symptoms are the predecessor to more severe heart disease.

Sir Dr. James Black had an eclectic array of employment ventures throughout his lifetime. In 1958, he was employed by ICI, Imperial Chemical Industries, as a senior pharmacologist. While employed at ICI, Black discovered the hormone epinephrine and norepinephrine increased heart contractions causing high blood pressure and consequently causing more stress to the heart muscle. In 1963, he created the drug called Propranolol. The genius behind this pharmaceutical innovation was its ability to block the hormone epinephrine and norepinephrine from attaching themselves to the heart muscle therefore allowing the heart the ability to slow down and pump blood more efficiently. This drug is also taken by patients that suffer from angina, migraine headaches, tremors, and panic attacks such as stage fright. Propranolol helps to calm the performer's heart rate, enabling them to effectively perform on stage. In 1964, he joined Smith Kline & French as head of research. In 1976, Dr. Black and his colleague Charon Robin Ganellin invented Cimetidine. It was popularly marketed as Tagamet. Tagamet's primary purpose was to prevent the histamine receptors that would increase secretion of gastric acid formations in the stomach and peptic ulcers. In 1976, Cimetidine was approved for useage in the United Kingdom and in 1979 the Food and Drug Administration approved its use by prescription in the United States. In 1973, he accepted the position of professor of pharmacology at University College, London. In 1978, he joined the Welcome Research Laboratories as director of therapeutic research. In 1984, he became a professor of Analytical Pharmacology at King's College, London. In 1993, he was appointed professor emeritus at King's College, London. From the period 1992-2006 he held the position of chancellor of the University of Dundee. To this day scientists are involved with discovering cures for cancer, diabetes and tropical diseases in the research facility named after Sir Dr. James Black at the University, which greatly improved the quality of life of the human race throughout the world. Through Dr. Black's pharmaceutical genius it is said he has saved the lives of more people on the earth than all the bedside physicians in the past century combined.

Throughout Black's lifetime he was the recipient of numerous illustrious awards for his contributions to improving the human condition.

- Lasker Award- 1976.
- The initial recipitiant of the Artois-Baillet Latour Foundation Health Prize- 1979.
- The Nobel Prize for Physiology or Medicine in 1988. That same year he formed the James Black Foundation. This was a not-for-profit organization that was established for scientists involved with new drug research.
- Royal Medal- 2004.

Dr. Black was also a member of the following academic societies throughout his lifetime:

- A Knight Bachelor by the Royal Crown on 10 February 1981 for services to medical research.
- Appointed to the Order of Merit in 2000.
- Fellow of the Royal Societies of London as well as Edinburgh.
- Member of the Royal College of Physicians.

On Monday 22 March 2010, Sir Dr. Black's death was announced by the University of Dundee. He died in London, England at the age of eighty-five.

Sir Dr. Black was light-years ahead of his contemporaries. Throughout the 1970's and 80's Dr. Black's discoveries spearheaded the rapid growth of the pharmaceutical industry. His efforts pioneered a culture of creativity and productivity in the field of pharmaceuticals that has continued to this present day.

It has been said, medicine is one part art and one part the science of healing. Through his innovative beta-blockers and peptic ulcer remedies Sir. Dr. Black changed the landscape of modern medicine practices.

Professor Dr. Ian Donald.

"Courtesy of Professor Asim Kurjak and the Ian Donald Inter-University School of Medical Ultrasound in Dubrovnik, Croatia."

## Professor Dr. Ian Donald

Born on 27 December 1910 in Liskeard, Cornwell, England.
Died on 19 June 1987 in Paglesham, Essex, England.
His family ancestry and linage are Scottish.


Inventor of the Ultrasound machine used in medicine.


It is only human nature for a parent to desire the best the world can offer for his or her child. More than any other time in the history of the world has prenatal care become such an indispensable component of Obstetrics. The Ultrasound has become the centerpiece of the modern day prenatal examination. This apparatus produces a black and white, grainy image of your unborn child that even the most trained eyes find difficult to decipher at times. The purpose behind the ultrasound is two fold: to assist physicians in detecting prenatal abnormalities and as the first image a parent-to-be will ever see of their unborn child. This is the story of how it all began.

You could say Dr. Donald's family business was medicine. He was a son and grandson of Scottish doctors. Education was placed at high regard within the Donald Clan. As a child young Donald attended the Warriston School in Moffat and the prestigious Fettes College in Edinburgh. He then emigrated with his family to South Africa, where he completed his bachelor degree at Diocesan College in Cape Town. Returning to London he then attended medical school at St. Thomas Hospital, graduating in 1937.

When the Second World War erupted in 1939 he joined the Royal Air Force Medical Division. While a member of the RAF stationed in the Hebrides, Dr. Donald first gained experience with the technology behind the SONAR and RADAR. For his gallant efforts rescuing fellow injured airmen from burning fighter planes still loaded with armaments, Donald was granted the honor of MBE, Most Excellent Order of the British Empire for his distinguished service. At the conclusion of the war he returned to St. Thomas Hospital of London as a qualified obstetrician in 1947.

In 1954 Dr. Donald was appointed Regius Chair and Professor of Obstetrics and Gynecology at the Glasgow University where he stayed until 1976. In 1955, he began his ultrasound research. While employed at St. Thomas Hospital Dr. Donald gained the acquaintance of Thomas Brown C Eng MIEE. At the time of their first encounter, Brown whom was born in Glasgow in 1933 was employed as an engineer with Kelvin & Hughes in Hillington, working on industrial ultrasounds. While employed by Kelvin & Hughes, his duties predominantly involved regulating sensitivity levels on modified sonar devices that were used during the Second World War, but only smaller. These machines would later evolve into the modern ultrasound machine. During these early experiments conducted in 1955 Dr. Donald and his team primarily and exclusively used the Henry Hughes Mk2 flaw detector. The flaw detectors primary responsibility was to attempt to spot cysts and other abnormalities in the abdomen and brain.

Donald with the assistance of Brown, soon arrived at the assertion soft tissue tumors beneath the skin were difficult to detect using conventional x-rays and therefore a new cost effective, non-invasive, alternative soon became their primary motivation. Together with Dr. John MacVicar, a fellow Scottish obstetrician, they set off to create a more comprehensive ultrasound diagnostic machine. Their explorations and discoveries were published in *The Lancent*, a weekly peer-reviewed general medical journal, on 7 June 1958, under the title: *Investigation of Abdominal Masses by Pulsed Ultrasound*. Until today this document is recognized as one of the most important papers ever written on the subject of diagnostic medical imaging. Through their perseverance and diligent efforts they developed the world's first safe, painless, reliable, ultrasound diagnostic machine in 1958. The primary reason behind the unbounded success of the ultrasound machine is the fact when an image of a healthy organ is produced such as a kidney, a liver, or a uterus, it is displayed as hallow. Therefore if a malignancy is detected it is shown as a solid mass. In addition, the released sound waves do not infected benign organs or an unborn fetus. In 1976, Thomas Brown also developed the world's first three-dimensional ultrasound scanner.

By 1959, the father of Obstetric Ultrasound began to focus his creative energies towards his primary field of expertise, maternity and prenatal care. Throughout his life Dr. Donald achieved worldwide recognition for his innovative discoveries. He was received by the Queen Mother during the opening of the Queen Mother's Hospital in Glasgow in 1964.

He also met His Holiness Pope John Paul II in 1976 to discuss the changing perceptions of the unborn fetus. Due to the ultrasounds unabashed reception by mothers-to-be in the surrounding hospitals of Glasgow during these early days, within a few years ultrasound screening became common place during prenatal examinations.

Though the technology has been refined upon we must not forget the efforts of the brilliant men that brought the world the ultrasound.

On Friday 19 June 1987, Professor Dr. Ian Donald passed away. He was seventy-six years old. He was put to rest in the quiet country churchyard of St. Peters, Paglesham, Essex, England.

Alexander Muirhead.

"Courtesy of Bill Burns, Publisher & Webmaster: atlantic-cable.com

## Alexander Muirhead

The first person to ever successfully record a patient's heartbeat.

A heartbeat is measured with electrical pulses and the EKG, Electrocardiogram is the devise that measures, evaluates and records such conditions. The EKG's primary function is to provide information about the electrical conduction of the heart, in other words its wiring. It supplies information that allows physicians the ability to detect any unseen damage to the heart or surrounding tissue. Several examples of abnormalities that may occur within the heart are as followed: a heart beat may be either too fast or too slow or the muscle may be producing insufficient amounts of oxygen, thus causing an unforeseen heart attack.

Alexander Muirhead was born on Friday 26 May 1848, in Salton, East Lothian, Scotland to Margaret Lauder and John Muirhead. As a young adult he attended University College in London where he excelled in the disciplines of Chemistry and Mathematics. In 1869, he received a Bachelor of Science in Chemistry with distinctions. Soon after completing his Bachelor of Science requirements he gained employment at St. Bartholomew Hospital. This is where he began his life-long journey in Electrical Standards. While completing his post-graduate studies at St. Bartholomew Hospital: 1869-1870, Muirhead performed the worlds first recorded EKG, though the claim has been disputed. While employed at St. Bartholomew he was responsible for the care of a feverish patient.

101

Muirhead decided to record the patient's heartbeat in the attempt to discover the root of his ailment. He attached wires to the patient's wrists then connected them to an apparatus called the Lippmann Capillary Electrometer. The Electrometer was then connected to a projector to measure and record the electrical image of the heart on a photograph plate.

The EKG was not the only innovation Muirhead was involved with during his lifetime. In 1872, soon after completing his Doctoral of Science in Electrical Engineering he became the scientific advisor for his father's firm. His father, John Muirhead originally was a farmer who soon became enticed by the bright lights of London. In London he opened a cable telegraphy company with his partner Latimer Clark on Regency Street, Westminster, London. As an Electrical Engineer and Physicist, Alexander secured patents in duplexing telegraph signals that would be used in submarine cables. He was also a member of the creative group headed by Sir Oliver Lodge responsible for developing the wireless telegraph. He later sold his tuning patents to the Marconi Company in 1912. He was also a member of several prestigious intellectual societies: the Chemical Society 1870, he was one of the inaugural members of the Physical Society of London 1874, The Institution of Electrical Engineering and Technology 1877, and a Fellow of the Royal Society 1904.

Throughout the years technology has improved and transformed Muirhead's original crude concept of the EKG machine which was not widely in use until 1911, into one of the most vital pieces of medical equipment in a modern hospital setting today. Alexander Muirhead died on Monday 13 December 1920, in Shortlands, Kent, England at the age of seventy-two. He is buried in West Norwood Cemetery, London.

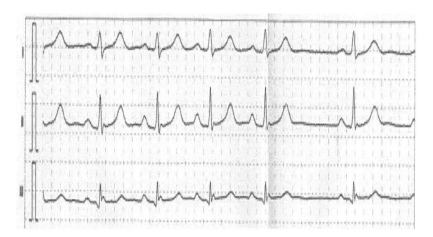

Electrocardiogram Tracing.

Sir James Young Simpson.

"Courtesy of the College Library, the Royal College of Surgeons of Edinburgh."

## Sir James Young Simpson

He introduced the Anaesthesia Chloroform into medical use during childbirth.

James Simpson was born on Friday 7 June 1811 in the picturesque town of Bathgate, West Lothian, Scotland. He was the youngest of seven children born to Mary and David Simpson, a baker by trade. At a young age his parents soon recognized his superior scholastic and cognitive capabilities. At the unassuming age of fourteen years old, young James was enrolled into the University of Edinburgh. Around this time while studying at University James added the middle name Young. He never formally penned his feelings on why he made the addition but some opinions suggest that it was due to his premature age at the time he graduated from medical college. Only five years after entering the University of Edinburgh he graduated at the age of nineteen. But due to of his unadvanced age he had to wait two additional years after his commencements to properly receive his license to practice medicine in 1832. Soon after, Dr. Simpson whom it was said possessed enormous energy for the vocation of Obstetrics began his life-long journey that would change the course of modern medicine.

In 1835, he was nominated senior president of the Royal Society of Edinburgh. In 1839, at twenty-eight years of age he was appointed professor and chair of Midwifery Obstetrics at the University of Edinburgh. Dr. Simpson was always a champion for patient safety and wellness throughout his life. During this time in the world there was very little a physician could do to relieve his patience's pain.

105

Therefore a very large portion of society avoided surgeries of any kind. Around the year 1847, he along with several colleagues began to experiment with different chemicals in the hope of uncovering ways to diminish some of the discomforts of surgery and childbirth. It is widely accepted on the night of 4 November 1847, Dr. Simpson and two colleagues Dr. George Keith and Dr. Matthew Duncan, retired to his dinning room on 52 Queen Street to do some research in the attempt to discover a substitute to Ether. That night the trio conducted experiments by testing an array of enigmatic chemicals on themselves. After testing the chemicals on themselves they planned to record their findings for future analysis. On that particular night the three scientists partook in the inhaling of a chemical called Chloroform. Their initial reactions after inhaling the Chloroform were sensations of relaxation, delight and joy. Then suddenly the trio became light-headed and slipped into unconsciousness. They fortunately awoke the next morning to the realization that they had stumbled upon a very potent narcotic. Just by sure luck the three did not cause themselves any severe illness or possible death with their initial dosage. A little more and they might have caused themselves cardiac arrest, coma or possible death. Too little and they might have felt its medical abilities were nonexistent. With expertise in Midwifery, Simpson soon recognized Chloroform could be an ideal Anaesthesia to relieve the pains of labour during childbirth.

Following the discovery of Chloroform Dr. Simpson was encompassed with great opposition predominantly from the Calvinist church. Their contention derived from their beliefs originated from the Old Testament's story of Eve. They believed due to Eve's transgressions, childbirth should forever be brought forth with great pain. In addition, they felt society should not go against the will of God. Interestingly enough until today there are pockets of the population that still hold on to these belief. They believe the administering of painkillers during childbirth may in some way cause unnecessary harm to the unborn child. But what these detractors have neglected to mention or recognize are the possibilities of unnecessary traumas the unborn may endure during the process of childbirth. Chloroform used as a painkiller during childbirth did not gain world-wide acceptance until Queen Victoria agreed to be given the wonder-drug during the birth of her son Prince Leopold in 1853. With the approval of the Queen, the public gradually accepted the benefits of Simpson's Anaesthesia.

As gratitude for his contributions within the discipline of medicine, Dr. Simpson was given several hounorable distinctions throughout his life. He was commissioned a Baronet of Strathavon in the county of Linlithgow and in the City of Edinburgh in 1866. In the same year he was also the first person ever to be knighted solely based on his contributions within the field of medicine. Though chloroform remained his greatest contribution to medicine, to the masses that he cared for he was revered as a kind, genital, sympathetic doctor who few can compare. On Friday 6 May 1870, at the age of fifty-eight Dr. Simpson died in his home in Edinburgh, he was placed to rest within his family grave near his home and where he toiled his life's work, Warriston Cemetery. A burial site was offered at Westminster Abby though his family declined the suggestion. On the day of his funeral it was proclaimed a National Holiday throughout Scotland.

Dr. Alexander Wood.

"Courtesy of David Pearce and www.general-anaesthesia.com"

## Dr. Alexander Wood

Inventor of the Hypodermic Syringe.

The word hypodermic derives from the Greek word for under the skin. A hypodermic syringe is a piston syringe that is fitted with a hollow needle to inject medicine below the skin or draw from it.

Dr. Wood's was born on Wednesday 10 December 1817, in Cupar, Fife, Scotland. He was the son of Dr. James Wood and Mary Wood, whom were both cousins. Education was held with great esteem in the Wood household. Therefore it is not a surprise his pursuit of higher learning began at a very early age. The first educational institution Wood attended was a private school in Edinburgh lead by Mr. Hindnarsh By 1826, at the age of nine he was attending the prestigious Edinburgh Academy. He remained a student there until 1832. At the age of fifteen, he entered Edinburgh University. On 1 August 1839, at the age of twenty-two he was accepted into medical school. During this time in world history Edinburgh was the medical capital of Europe, therefore Wood's admittance into Edinburgh University brought with it much prestige. After his medical school training was complete, his first employment was as a medical officer with the Stockbridge Dispensary, soon followed by employment with the Royal Public Dispensary of

New Town. In 1850, he was appointed Secretary of the Royal College of Physicians of Edinburgh.

In 1853, at the age of thirty-six he invented the hypodermic syringe. The breakthrough of the syringe allowed physicians the ability to administrate medication directly into a patient's bloodstream. As in nature, positive intentions can some times turn negative. Dr. Wood's intention for his invention was for it to positively enrich the lives of the people that used it. His hypodermic syringe was initially used to administer Morphia as a painkiller to the patience under his care. He published his discoveries describing his new innovation in the Edinburgh Medical and Surgical Journal, 1855: "*A New Method for Treating Neuralgia by the Direct Application of Opiates to Painful Points*". Within the Journal's pages he described the vast amount of alternate potential uses for the hypodermic syringe.

Ironically enough, his wife Rebecca Massey is identified as the first addict of intravenous morphine. She eventually died of an overdose delivered by her husband's invention. Interestingly, she outlived her husband by ten years. She died in 1894.

Dr. Wood died on Tuesday 26 February 1884 at the age of sixty-six.

Loose estimates suggest about twenty-four billion syringes are used worldwide each year, with the around seven billion being used in the United States alone.

110

James Lind.

## James Lind

Developed the theory that citrus fruits would cure Scurvy.
The father of Nautical Medicine.

James Lind was a physician that specialized in
preventive medicine. During the time Lind walked the earth the high seas
were considered the great frontier, the bastion of immeasurable fortune
and glory. Lind was known as a physician and advocate focusing on
improving the working conditions on and within British war ships. His
life's work primarily focused on the improved hygienic conditions of
sailors within the Royal Navy. The primary tool imposed by Lind to
combat the unsanitary conditions within the Royal Navy was a process of
fumigating the below deck quarters of the war ships, primarily focusing
on the sailors clothing and bedding with the use of a combination of
sulfur and arsenic.

James Lind was born on Monday 4 October 1716 in
Edinburgh, Scotland, to prosperous merchant parents named Margaret
Smelum and James Lind. In 1731, at the age of fifteen he began his
medical apprenticeship under the tutelage of George Langlands. In 1739,
at the age of twenty-three he entered the Royal Navy as a surgeon's mate
serving in the Mediterranean Sea off the coast of West Africa and the
West Indies. In 1747, at thirty-one years of age he became a surgeon on
the HMS Salisbury. The HMS Salisbury was part of the formation of
warships stationed in defense of the English Channel. It was widely
known throughout the medical community at the time Scurvy was the

caused of more deaths to the British Naval Fleet than the entire French and Spanish Armadas could inflict combine. This conclusion became the premise behind Lind's experimental trials relating to the prevention and spread of Scurvy. Scurvy is a disease that results from a deficiency of ascorbic acid, the chemical name for Vitamin C. Some visual symptoms of this deficiency are as followed, bleeding gums, and teeth and hair loss. The unfortunate prognosis for these symptoms if left untreated is convulsions and or possibly death.

While patrolling on the Bay of Biscay, Lind conducted the first formal clinically controlled tests regarding the prevention and spread of Scurvy. His experiments were based upon research performed by Johann Bachstrom in 1734 that suggested the symptoms of Scurvy were caused by an absence of fresh vegetables in the diet. In which would become exasperated during long sea voyages where food rations did not include fresh fruit or vegetables. During this time in naval history salted meats such as preserve beef and pork were the predominant food supply on long voyages at sea. Lind began his experiment by choosing twelve sailors whom were presently suffering from Scurvy on the Salisbury. He then separated the sailors into six pairs. Along with their daily food rations some groups were supplied with cider, while others were given seawater, others were supplied combinations of garlic, mustard and horseradish, while others still were treated with a diet that included oranges and lemons. The mariners that were fed a diet of oranges and lemons quickly recovered from their symptoms of Scurvy while the sailors that were not offered the citrus rations either did not show any improvement regarding their symptoms or gradually worsened. It should be mentioned in order to obtain optimal results from citrus fruit consumption the fruit must be eaten fresh. The fruit should also not be heated, such as in a tea. The conclusions reveled from Lind's experiments demonstrated that a diet that included citrus fruits greatly reduced the probability of contracting Scurvy. Another dietetic improvement Lind promoted was the practice of boiling distilling sea water to produce fresh drinkable water.

Soon after arriving at his conclusions for reducing the spread of Scurvy he left the Navy. In 1748, Lind returned to the University of Edinburgh to pursue the completion his Medical Degree. The only requirement lacking from his credentials was a doctoral thesis. For the topic of his thesis he chose the subject of venereal lesions. It has been documented that his thesis apparently was written in haste and by all historical accounts a trivial work at best. But with all its flaws it was sufficient none the less for the board to issue Lind his license to practice medicine. He received his degree and license to practice medicine that same year, primarily based on his past experiences and medical knowledge obtained during his days on the high seas. Later that same year he married his cousin Isobel Dickie. During his lifetime he also wrote two books: *A Treatise of the Scurvy* in 1753 and *An Essay on the Most Effective Means of Preserving the Health of Seamen in the Royal Navy* in 1757.

In 1768, he also published *An Essay on Disease Incidental to Europeans in Hot Climates.* This became the leading resources for information regarding tropical medicine for the next fifty years.

In 1758, he was appointed as the chief physician of the Royal Navy Hospital at Gosport, in the south of England. He was succeeded by his son and assistant John after twenty-five years of service in 1783.

James Lind died on Sunday 13 July 1794 in Gosport, England at the age of seventy-seven. Unfortunately his findings were not widely acted upon by the Royal British Navy until 1795, when they began to issue lemon juice to each ships basic ration supply. The term Limies referring to British sailors derives from Lind's dietetic discoveries.

James Lind will forever be remembered for his tireless work to improve and preserve the health and lives of ordinary men.

117

Andrew Carnegie.

"Courtesy of the Andrew Carnegie Birthplace Museum, Dunferline, Scotland."

## Andrew Carnegie

A Philanthropist, patron of libraries and higher learning, advocate of world peace and billionaire.

It is said a true Scotsman is shrewd with his pennies, but generous with his millions. So can be said of Andrew Carnegie.

Throughout the years there have been countless volumes written validating Carnegie's steel empire legacy. But these pages will focus upon his philanthropic efforts and how his generosity contributed to improve our modern society. Andrew Carnegie was born on Wednesday 25 November 1835, in the medieval capital of Scotland, Dunfirmline, to a family of humble means. Though his family was not blessed with material wealth, they were able to provide him with the gifts of a strong family unit and an appreciation of the Scottish culture. From an early age young Andrew was taught that the path to contentment in life would undoubtedly emanate from the pursuit of higher education. He also had a keen understanding of the man working on his factory floor and what that man wanted out of his life and his family's lives. He understood that these men wanted more for their children and their children's children. He also understood that the only way for upward mobility to occur in ones life was through education. He also understood the plight of the underprivileged and the disadvantaged. He knew that it was the moral responsibility of the populous blessed into positions of privilege to give back to society, financially or otherwise.

In the words of Carnegie himself, "There is no class so pitiably wretched as that which possesses money and nothing else."

As an avid promoter of education and more specifically the spread of the English language through spelling reform, library construction soon became the cornerstone of his philanthropic endeavors. With a collaboration of public lands and Carnegie's endowments, over twenty-five hundred libraries from 1883 to 1929 were built throughout the United Kingdom, the United States and other English speaking countries throughout the world. The Carnegie foundation kept the process for library construction very streamlined. The neighborhood of interest would first submit their building design proposal. If the proposal was granted approval construction on the facility would commence. There were two essential mandatory elements for design approval. First, all structures needed to possess a front door stairway for entrance, symbolizing elevation to higher learning. The other concession required was a light source centered near the entrance such as a lamppost, lantern or some other form of illumination. This represented enlightenment. The cornerstone for the last public library built with Carnegie money was set on 28 June 1923 in Woodhaven, Queens, New York. It opened its doors less than seven months later on 7 January 1924.

Carnegie launched his philanthropic crusade while he was still fully engrossed as the reining steel tycoon of the world. As so eloquently articulated by Glinda the Good Witch, "It's always best to start at the beginning," and that was exactly where Carnegie began his audacious endeavor, in his hometown of Dunfirnline, Scotland.

His first donation to his hometown was in 1879, when he orchestrated the construction of a public swimming-bath facility and in 1883 with his first free public library. In 1884, he donated fifty thousand dollars to build the Carnegie Laboratory at Bellevue Hospital Medical College, presently part of New York University Medical Center. In 1885, the patron of libraries donated five hundred thousand dollars to Pittsburgh to build a public library. In 1886, he donated two hundred, fifty thousand dollars to Allegheny City to build a music hall and library. That same year in Edinburgh, Carnegie donated two hundred, fifty thousand pounds for a free library for the city. In 1899, he donated fifty thousand dollars to establish the University of Birmingham. As an avid proponent of laissez-faire forms of government and the idea of ones right to free will, you can appreciate his sentiments towards the end of the Spanish-American War in 1898, when the United States bought the Philippines from Spain for twenty million dollars. Carnegie was of the opinion this was an order of imperialism set forth by the United States toward the Philippines. He proposed to give the Philippines that same amount, twenty million dollars, to buy their freedom from the U.S. Though nothing even became of his gesture, it exemplified Carnegie's anti-imperialistic sentiments. This experience was the springboard to the Carnegie Council on Ethics and International Affairs. Initially established in 1914 as the Church Peace Union, it promoted ethical practices in respect to international affairs.

"I resolve to stop accumulating and begin the infinitely more serious and difficult task of wise distribution." Carnegie

By 1901, Carnegie was sixty-six years of age. With retirement looming he agreed to an unprecedented amount of four hundred, eighty million dollars from the American banker J.P. Morgan for the purchase of his steel company. That exorbitant amount of money is estimated to be worth over thirteen billion dollars, adjusted for present inflation. This transaction between the two tycoons became the largest personal commercial transaction to date. It also established the first corporation, The United States Steel Corporation, in recorded world history. Soon began a new chapter in Andrew Carnegie's celebrated life, fulltime Philanthropy. In 1901, he established the Carnegie Trust for Universities throughout Scotland. Credited with a deed signed on 7 June 1901, and incorporated the following year by Royal Charter this was an endowment of ten million pounds initially issued to the four University sites, Edinburgh, Glasgow, Aberdeen and St. Andrews-Dundee, in the amount of fifty thousand pounds annually. As more university sites were established they would also be included within the endowment. The predominant purpose for these funds was to bolster research in the sciences and to increase accessibility to university for qualified and merited potential students of Scotland. As gratitude for his donations to the universities of Scotland he was elected Lord Rector of the University of St. Andrews. During that year he also donated two million dollars to establish the Carnegie Institute of Technology in Pittsburgh, presently part of Carnegie-Mellon University.

The following year he donated another two million dollars to establish the Carnegie Institute in Washington D.C., focusing on research in the disciplines of natural and physical sciences. In addition that same year a pension fund was established for the former employees of Homestead Steel Works. The motivation behind this endowment originated in 1888 when Carnegie bought the Homestead Steel Works. In 1892, members of the steel union, The Amalgamated Association of Iron and Steel workers, requested higher wages from Carnegie. When management refused their requests the workers were then locked out of work. Protests by the workers soon ensued. Strikebreakers were subsequently hired by management. With tensions mounting on 6 July, a fight erupted between security hired by management and striking workers. As a result of the mayhem ten men, seven strikers and three Pinkerton security agents were killed while hundreds other were injured. In order to calm the proceeding disorder the Governor of Pennsylvania was forced to order two brigades of state militia to resume the peace. Though all of the forerun events occurred while Carnegie was on holiday in Scotland, his business reputation was forever tarnished from what had transpired. In 1902, Carnegie bought Pittencrief Park in Dunfermline, Fife, and then opened the park for public use. The Dunfermline Carnegie Trust was established the following year for the purpose of maintaining the property. In addition to maintaining the museum of Carnegie's birthplace and all that is Carnegie in Dunfermline.

Carnegie was also a great supporter of the Tuskegee Institute headed by Booker T. Washington. Beginning in 1903, he donated one million, three hundred thousand dollars with an additional twenty thousand dollars reserved for the construction of a library on its campus. His endowment continued through 1963 when his foundation gave one million, five hundred thousand dollars to the United Negro College Fund. In 1903, the Carnegie Endowment of International Peace donated one-million five-hundred thousand dollars for the construction of The Hague Palace of Peace. This is home to the World Court in the Netherlands. The primary focus of this organization was to investigate the scientific underlining reasoning behind wars, then with hope ultimately finding a way to abolish war from our collective consciousness. That same year the International Bureau of American Republics received a one hundred, fifty thousand dollar endowment for the construction of their central office, the Pan-American Palace located in Washington D.C. In 1904, he founded the Carnegie Hero Funds in the United States and Canada. Several years later the endowment stretched to include the United Kingdom, Switzerland, Norway, Sweden, France, Italy, The Netherlands, Belgium, Denmark, and Germany. In 1905, he established a retirement fund for American college professors, later it was renamed the TIAA-CREF. In 1911, his foundation contributed ten million dollars for the construction of the Hooker Telescope on the Carnegie Institution campus. In 1913, a ten million dollar endowment created the Carnegie United Kingdom Trust.

This organizations primary responsibility was to provide grants to institutions and organizations encouraging the promotion of libraries, village halls, parks, youth projects, community development projects, the arts and environmental causes. As his philanthropic endeavors grew additional external organizations were established to better serve the needs of the grant recipients. The largest of these organizations was the Carnegie Corporation of New York. Throughout the years since its inception it has aided colleges and other academic institutions to the amount of one hundred twenty-five million dollars in endowments. He also financed the construction of over seven thousand pipe organs for churches throughout the United States and Great Britain and one can not forget the Carnegie Hall built in 1890 situated on Seventh Avenue, between Fifty-Sixth Street and Fifty-Seventh Street. If you want to get there, practice, practice, practice.

Carnegie was convinced the future leaders of the earth would derive from corners of the world where nothing is given or promised and where oncs relentless will to succeed thrives. He also felt it was counter productive for wealthy parents to leave robust inheritances to their children. His opinion was that it was a better idea to donate ones monetary resources to benefit the greater good of the human race. At the age of eighty-three, Andrew Carnegie succumbed to bronchial pneumonia and died on Monday 11 August 1919. He was buried at the Sleepy Hollow Cemetery in Tarrytown, New York.

Some men change the world with an invention or with a modification to a preexisting invention, while others as Andrew Carnegie, altered the landscape with their wealth and influence. He was a man whom truly embodied the American dream, an immigrant who went from rags to riches.

As the eons pass Andrew Carnegie will hopefully be remembered not just as a billionaire steel tycoon, but rather as a man who impacted innumerable lives with his foresight and generosity more than any other man in the last one hundred years.

"This signature is believed to be ineligible for copyright and therefore in the public domain because it falls below the required level of originality for copyright protection both in the United States and in the source country (if different). In this case, the source country (e.g. the country of nationality of the signatory) is believed to be Scotland."

John Napier.

"Courtesy of Wellcome Library, London."

## John Napier

1550- 4 April 1617

Inventor of Logarithms and popularized the use of the Decimal Point.

John Napier is considered by many to be the first Scottish born person to make a significant contribution within the scientific community. Napier was born into Scottish nobility, a baron with the title the 7th Laird of Merchiston at Merchiston Tower Edinburgh, Scotland. He attended St. Andrews University, though left prior to completing his degree. Following his time at University around 1564, he traveled extensively throughout Europe gaining much knowledge and worldly experience. Napier's life's work was spent as a Theologian and Mathematician. But his immorality derives from his unwavering pursuit to improve the human condition. He considered Mathematics his hobby, while an ardent Protestant and anti-catholic, theology was his passion. In the book he wrote in 1593 titled: *A plaine discovery of the whole Revelation of St. John*, he attempted to utilize the number scattered throughout the book of Revelations to predict the precise year the world would end. Throughout his extensive research he concluded the world's demise would occur either in the years 1688 or 1700. Compounding this inaccuracy, he also stated that he had discovered Pope Clement VIII was the Antichrist. Pope Clement VIII was the Pope at the time Napier wrote his book. Though his conclusions were grossly incorrect, by publishing his book he became the first person born in Scotland to interpret biblical scriptures and put his findings to paper. Throughout his lifetime Napier considered the publication of this book his most crowning achievement.

Strangely enough during Napier's lifetime unsavory rumors spread about his odd activities and unworldly intelligence perceived by some of his peers. Some even suggested he was in league with the Devil. One of these exaggerations derived from Napier's frequent late night walks in his nightgown and cap along his estate grounds. Another rumor was caused by his grass being vastly greener than surrounding estates. His defense for the later was that his greener grass was due to his agricultural prowess and nothing more. There is also the story of how Napier used a black rooster to ascertain a thieving servant. As the story goes, one of his servants allegedly stole some tools from one of Napier's sheds. So the Warlock summoned all his servants to stand around him. He then began to explain that he had a black rooster that possessed magical powers of divination and subsequently the power to discover the true thief. He then instructed the servants to enter the shed. He then instructed each servant to rub the back of the bird and then come out of the shed. What the clever scientist didn't tell the unassuming crew was that prior to him summoning the lot to the shed he covered the rooster with lamp soot. Therefore whoever touched the Devil Bird would emerge with hands of black. Therefore, if you were innocent of the accusations you would not hesitate to rub the bird, though if you were guilty you would not have the nerve to touch the rooster. So when all the servants exited the shed they were instructed to present their hands to their master. The clean handed servant was the thief. Was John Napier clever? Indeed! Demonic? Probably not. Today, John Napier is commonly known for his contributions within the discipline of Mathematics.

During the time of his life, Astronomy was gaining popularity. But what stifled most astronomers of the time was the laborious mathematical calculations. "There is nothing….that is so troublesome to mathematical practice….than the multiplication, division, square and cubical extractions of great numbers,….I began therefore to consider in my mind by what certain and ready art I might remove these hindrances…."., from the authors preface in *A Italic Description of the Admirable Table of Logarithms*, first published in 1616. It also should be remembered, during this period of world history people thought the world not the sun was at the center of the Solar System and that the earth was flat. Included in this line of thought were the views and opinions of the Pope. We must be aware this was also a world without calculators and computers. In some cases mathematical calculations might have taken teams of scientists' days even perhaps weeks to complete. Napier's logarithms, which he invented in 1614 allowed for large mathematical problems to be solved in a fraction of the time, in addition to reducing the possibility of human error. In his published works of 1614: *Mirifici logarithmorum canonis descriptio*, which means *A Description of the Wonderful Table of Logarithms*, Napier illustrates the technical principals and benefits of using logarithms. Napier was also responsible for advancing the concept of the decimal point. The decimal point allowed real numbers smaller than one to be computed at a faster rate, while also reducing the margin of human error. He also invented the world's first calculating devise, Napier's bones.

Alexander Shanks.

## Alexander Shanks

The inventor of the first non-human drawn lawnmower.

Alexander Shanks was born on Monday 16 February 1801 in Milnetown of Bridgetown, Forfarshire, Scotland. This is near the present-day hamlet of Douglastown. If there was one commodity Scotland possesses in abundance it would undoubtedly be the lush grass that blankets her majestic hillsides and awe-inspiring valleys. Prior to Shanks invention of the first non-human drawn lawnmower there were only three ways for grass to be cut, with the use of a scythe, a sickle or by the labor of sheep. Therefore it was inevitable one of Scotland's sons would create a machine that would be able to manicure its magnificent terrain. The birth of this invention arrived with Shanks commission in 1841 to build a lawnmower for the William Fullerton Lindsey Carnegie of Kimblethmont Estate in Baysack. So Shanks and his sons soon began to construct his new invention inside their factory at Ogilvy Place in Arbroath. This would become the world's first non-human drawn lawnmower. The way this machine operated was the controller of the apparatus would guide a pony in front of the lawnmower in order to cut the grass. Shanks' pony driven lawnmower built in 1841 had a 27" base. The next year he built one with a 42" wide base that could be drawn by a horse. During that same year 1842, Shanks was granted a patent for his Grass Cutting Machine. This was the first patent ever issued for a grass cutting devise of any capacity.

133

To this day the company Shanks began in Arbroath still supplies the lawnmowers that cut the grass at Wimbledon, the cricket grounds at Lords, and the Old Course at St. Andrews. The machine Shanks created over one hundred seventy years ago is a direct predecessor to the modern-day motorized lawnmower. Interestingly enough even today you can still see his invention in use in countries such as India.

Edwin Budding of England, is ordinarily attributed with inventing the first hand powered, push lawnmower. He patented his invention on 31 August 1830. He is also credited with inventing the adjustable spanning wrench. A tool found in just about every toolbox around the world.

After passing away at the young age of forty-four years old on Friday 19 September 1845, Alexander Shanks was placed to rest in the graveyard of the Church of Scotland in Kirkliston. After his death his sons took over the business. They gave a demonstration of their father's invention; the 42" machine called the Shanks five-drummer at the Crystal Palace Exposition of London of 1851 and with patience and care developed a successful business that has carried on through until the twenty-first century.

The euphemism: Shanks's Pony meaning to travel by foot possibly derives from the popularity of Alexander's pony-drawn lawnmower. While other schools of thought suggest the meaning of the euphemism can be traced to the late eighteenth century in Robert Fergusson's *Poems on Various Subjects,* 1774: "He took shanks-naig, but fient may care." Also the lower portion of the leg is defined as the shin or shank.

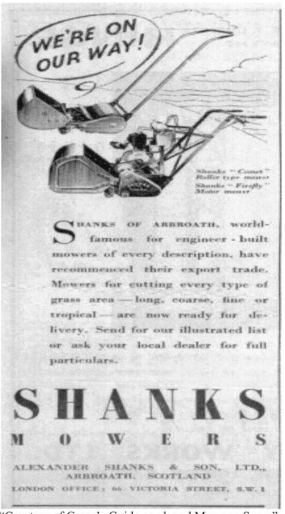

"Courtesy of Grace's Guide.co.uk and Maryann Soper"

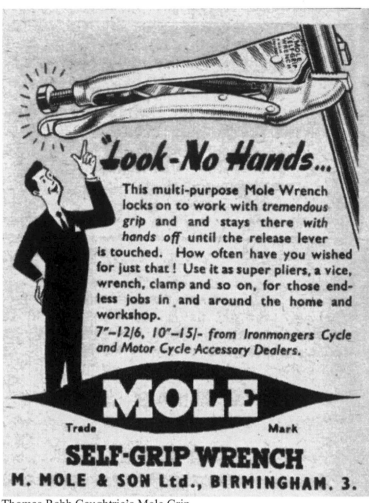

Thomas Robb Coughtrie's Mole Grip.

## Thomas Robb Coughtrie

He was an electrical engineer that patented the Mole Grip/Vice Grip Pliers.


No toolbox is complete without a pair of Mole Grip/Vice Grip Pliers. The genius that makes this tool such a viable addition is its versatility. The Mole Grip/Vice Grip Pliers is a cross between pliers, a wrench and a clamp. Whether you are doing repairs on your car, carpentry, to medal work, the Mole Grip adheres to every job. The assembly of this tool has not changed since its conception. Birthed from cast steel, one handle has a screw at the end. The other hand has a fast release lever to allow the user to quickly unfasten the clamp and move unto the next assignment. A debate has erupted regarding who first actually came up with the concept for this tool. The Vice-Grip locking pliers were developed and patented in 1921 and 1924 in the United States by a Danish immigrant whom settled in DeWitt Nebraska named Vilhelm "Bill" Peterson. The Vice-Grip is the American brand for this tool. Thomas Coughtrie was issued his patent for the British version called the Mole-Grip, self-grip wrench in 1955. There are several variations of the Mole Grip/Vice-Grip sold throughout the world, but all serve similar purposes.

Thomas Robb Coughtrie was born on Sunday 25 November 1917, in Motherwell, Lanarkshire, Scotland to Mr. and Mrs. W. Jardine Coughtrie. He completed his formal education at Bellshill Academy. At the completion of his formal education he was qualified as a chartered engineer.

He gained employment as an engineer with M. Mole & Sons LTD. in 1947. When the second Mole brother passed away in 1950 he was appointed Managing Director of the company. After retiring from Mole & Sons in the late 1970's, he became the owner and Managing Director of Cardol Engineering Co. LTD. of Ponlypool, Wales, just outside Newport.

Thomas Coughtrie also played a vital role during the most important mission and perhaps one of the greatest engineering feats of the Second World War, the D-Day invasions of Normandy, France. During the days and months prior to the invasion the Electrical Engineer's primary responsibilities involved assisting in the installing, inspecting and maintaining of the top secret one thousand ton "Whales". The term "Whale" was the code name used for the flexible, floating, and six-mile roadway that connected the artificial Mulberry Harbour together.

The Mulberry Harbour was a pre-fabricated artificial harbour built during World War II to move supplies and armaments for the Allied Forces into position to begin the liberation movement of Western Europe out of Nazi control. The reason behind its construction was due to Germany's occupation of all the French ports making it virtually impossible for Allied Forces to ship any supplies to the battle front. Britain's solution to this dilemma was simple and very complicated at the same time. Construction commenced under a shroud of secrecy. Code names were created for each component of the construction in addition to the creation of false work orders.

138

These false work orders were put in place in order to detour spies from their true intentions. Over twenty-thousand workmen were used in the artificial harbours construction throughout England.

When completed the pieces of the Whales were then shipped over the English Channel to the coast of Normandy in preparation for the D-Day invasion. One was placed at Omaha Beach and the other was placed at Gold Beach.

After living an extraordinary life, Thomas Coughtrie passed away on Wednesday 27 August 2008 in Abergavenny Wales at the age of ninety.

One of the Mulberry Harbours.

Arthur James Arnot.

## Arthur James Arnot

The Electrical Engineer that patented the world's first Electric Drill.

You only have to take a look outside your window to spot the immense influence the Electric Drill has had on the modern world. Think of the countless structures that cover the earth that without the birth of the Electric Drill would have been forever trapped in the imagination of man. It is difficult to imagine a construction site without power tools and more specific the Electric Drill. Several examples of world altering structures the Electric Drill contributed in bringing into existence are as followed: the skyscraper, the bridge, tunnels, the construction of residential and commercial properties, everything inside these particular structures, the construction of trains, buses, automobiles, motorcycles, ship building, military and commercial aircraft, drilling for oil, mining for gold or precious medals, to the countless other objects covering the surface of he earth. Though the drill Arthur Arnot invented over one-hundred twenty years ago has greatly evolved, the premise behind his invention has remained virtually unchanged. Arnot's Electric Drill was predominantly used for drilling into large rocks. It was a cumbersome structure and not portable at all.

Arthur James Arnot was born on Saturday 26 August 1865 in Hamilton, Scotland to Elizabeth Helen McDonald and William Arnot, a commercial agent. Young Arthur was educated in Glasgow at the Hutchesontown Grammar School, the Haldane Academy and the West of Scotland Technical College.

His first employment after completing college was as an assistant engineer of the Grosvenor Gallery Power Station. In 1889, he moved to Melbourne Australia on a five year contract that lasted a wee bit longer to build an alternating current power plant. The following year he dipped his toe into immortality. On 20 August 1889, he was issued the patent for the world's first Electric Drill. Gradually gaining prominence and recognition for his labours he was appointed the first Electrical Engineer of the City of Melbourne in 1891 while at his post he was responsible for the installation of the city's first street light system: 1891-1892. In 1896, Arnot assisted in the drafting of the Victorian Electrical Light and Power Act. He also held several prominent positions with several other distinguished organizations. He was a member of the Institution of Electrical Engineers of London: 1899-1906. He was the President of the Electrical Association of New Wales and the Victorian Institute of Electrical Engineers: 1899. He was also the Counselor for Working Men's College: 1897-1901 and the Examiner of Electrical Technology for Victoria Technical Schools. From 1901 until 1929 when he retired, Arnot was employed as the Australian Manager for Babcock & Wilcox LTD, Sydney.

On Tuesday 15 October 1946, Arthur James Arnot passed away at the age of eighty-one in Castle Hill, New South Wales, Australia.

Since 1890 the Electric Drill has become the cornerstone of any respectable modern-day toolbox, while millions have been sold throughout the years.

George Bruce.

## George Bruce

He was a prosperous printer and inventor who patented typing fonts; printing typeface and borders.

It goes unnoticed when you spot a headline on the front page of a newspaper, an advertising movie poster, or the cover of this book. But the elements that motivates you to give that headline, movie or book title a second look is the font in which it is written. This is the brief story of one of the men whom carried typing fonts to your daily newspaper headlines.

George Bruce was born on Thursday 5 July 1781 in Edinburgh, Scotland. In 1795, at the age of fourteen years old he ventured to New York City in search of a better life and possibly his fame and fortune. Soon after his arrival in America he joined up with his older brother David. With his brother's assistance he acquired a book binding apprenticeship in Philadelphia, Pennsylvania. In 1798, soon after a yellow fever outbreak and his employer Thomas Dobson's Philadelphia office was destroyed by fire the brothers Bruce moved to Albany in pursuit of employment and a new beginning. Though with a lack of employment prospects they returned and settled in New York City within several months. In 1803, he secured employment with the Daily Advertiser, first as a foreman then as a printer and then as a publisher for the daily newspaper. In 1806, the brothers pooled their financial resources together and opened a book printing office at the corner of

Pearl Street and Coffeehouse Slip at the bottom of Wall Street. In 1809, they moved their operations to a larger location on Sloat Lane near Hanover Square. This area of New York City was known as Printing House Square and later the center of New York's commodity market. In 1812, Brother David ventured to England with the anticipation of learning the Stereotyping trade. Though upon returning to his shop on Sloat Lane he soon realized the techniques he was mentored in pertaining to Stereotyping in England were difficult to duplicate in the New World. Stereotyping was an early type of printing plate that could be used multiple times producing a similar printed image. It was ideally used for large production jobs such as newspaper printing. The mastery of Stereotyping was first invented in 1725 by a goldsmith born in Edinburgh named William Ged. It was later reintroduced with greater functionality in 1784 by Alexander Tillich born on Friday 23 February 1759, in Glasgow. Prior to this invention if a printer wanted to copy a document after the initial copies were complete he had to reset the original plates over again. This was not an economical process in time or money. The process William Ged used to create his Stereotyping Plates was to first to take a plaster mold of the documents page then cast it into metal to be able to be used multiple times in the future.

The following year the bothers opened Bruce Type Foundry, though due to his failing health older brother David soon retired from daily operations of the business thus dissolving their business partnership. In 1816, George moved the business operations of the foundry to Eldridge Street. Around 1832, George with the help of his nephew David Bruce Jr., invented a typecasting machine.

This machine soon became the printing industries standard until the turn of the twentieth century. On 9 November 1842, George Bruce was awarded the first design patent authorized by an Act of Congress in the history of the United States: U.S. patent D1. The patent was issued for typing fonts, printing typefaces and borders. Interestingly enough the patent issuing document was six hundred, sixty-six words in length.

Throughout the business community George was renowned for the personal attention he rendered to his customers and business associates alike. Dissimilar to many of his contemporaries he was recognized for his integrity, his benevolence and for being a great judge of character.

On Friday 6 July 1866, George Bruce passed away in New York City a wealthy man at the age of eighty-five. In 1877, his daughter donated fifty thousand dollars in her father's name to the City of New York for the construction of a public library furnished with books of every discipline. Completed in 1888, the original library was located on Forty-Second Street. In 1915, the library was relocated to its present location at 518 West 125th Street in Manhattan.

Samuel Wilson/ Uncle Sam.

"Courtesy of James Montgomery Flagg, artist. This image is a work of a U.S.
Military or Department of Defense employee, taken or made as part of that
person's official duties. As a work of the U.S. federal government, the image is
in the Public Domain."

## Samuel Wilson

He is the origin of the symbol of the United States of America, Uncle Sam.

The personification and one of the most iconic symbols of the United States of America, Uncle Sam has Scottish roots. The man behind the moniker was a descendent of one of the earliest families to settle in Boston, Massachusetts, Samuel Wilson. His connection to Scotland derives from his grandfather Robert Wilson, who was born in Greenock. Samuel Wilson was born to Lucy and Edward Wilson on Saturday 13 September 1766, in a town called Menotomy, presently called Arlington, part of the township of West Cambridge, Massachusetts. The circumstance that galvanized Wilson's immortality finds its origins with the role Samuel and his brother Ebenezer took during the War of 1812. During the War of 1812 the United States government was in need of increased amounts of provisions to feed her troops. The responsibility of securing these supplies fell upon the Secretary of War, William Eustris. He soon reached a contract with a supply company located in New York City headed by a man named Elbert Anderson Jr. He subsequently subcontracted the request to a slaughter house in Troy, New York called E&S Wilson, owned by brothers Ebenezer and Samuel. They were contracted to secure two thousand barrels of pork and three thousand barrels of beef for one year to be shipped to military cantonment located in Greenbush, New York as well as in New Jersey.

149

As the newly appointed meat inspector for the Northern Army, Samuel Wilson's responsibility was to secure the freshness and proper packaging of all shipped barrels of food. If a barrel was deemed of high quality, a stamp inscribed E.A.-U.S. would be placed on the barrel, E.A. indentified Elbert Anderson Jr., the contracted agent for the Northern Army and U.S. signified the United States. Inadvertently, the soldiers receiving the rations mistakenly thought the initials U.S. represented Uncle Sam, the nickname affectionately given to Samuel Wilson by the patrons of his slaughter house in Troy. As one of the pioneers of Troy, Samuel Wilson was considered in high regarded by the members of his community for his friendliness and fairness. From that point on the initials U.S. in association with military supplies would become synonymous with Uncle Sam.

The Real Uncle Sam died on Monday 31 July 1854 at the age of eighty-seven. He is buried in Oakwood Cemetery, Troy New York.

The only known image of Samuel Wilson/ Uncle Sam.

"Public Domain. Copyright has expired, life of the author plus 70 years in United States, United Kingdom and Australia."

The Signing of the United States Declaration of Independence.

## The United States Declaration of Independence.

Almost half the signers of the United States Declaration of Independence can claim ancestral roots deriving from Scotland. Two of the signers were even born in Scotland. James Wilson representing Pennsylvania was born in Carskerdo, Fifeshire, near St. Andrews on Tuesday 4 September 1742. He died at the age of fifty-five on 21 August 1798 in Eldenton, North Carolina. While Rev. John Witherspoon representing New Jersey was born in Gifford, Yester, in East Lothian, on Friday 5 February 1722. He died at the age of seventy-two on 15 November 1794 in Princeton, New Jersey. He was also the only clergyman to sign the American Declaration of Independence.

Scotland's Declaration of Arbroath was the model and the inspiration employed by Thomas Jefferson when he wrote the United States Declaration of Independence. Liberty, a tradition of freedom and the desire for sovereignty, resonated off the page of the letter sent to Pope John XXII on 6 April 1320. The United States Declaration of Independence consequently became the inspiration for other freedom movements throughout the world. Here are some examples of this such influence, The Manifesto of the Province of Flanders 1790, the Haitians in 1804, Venezuela 1811, the United Provinces of New Granada 1811, Argentine 1816, Chili 1818, Costa Rica 1821, El Salvador 1821, Guatemala 1821, Honduras 1821, Mexico 1821, Nicaragua 1821, Peru, 1821, Bolivia 1825, Uruguay 1825, Ecuador 1830, Columbia 1831, Paraguay 1842, Dominican Republic 1844, Libya 1847, Hungary 1849, New Zealand 1835, Confederate States of America 1860-1861, Czechoslovak 1918, Vietnam 1945, and Rhodesia 1965.

Scottish Hammer Throw.

"An illustration from *Round-About in Lands of Fact and Fancy.* This image is in the Public Domain because its copyright has expired. This applies to Australia, the European Union and those countries with a copyright term of life of the author plus seventy years."

**Sports & Athletics**

"There is an adage in sport participation that no matter how good a person is there always will be someone better. Perhaps it follows that no matter how much an individual knows there always is something more to learn." Foreman pg. 30.

**Shot Put, Hammer Throw, Weight Throw:**

The modern world of athletics is a milti-billion dollar enterprise, with no other nation contributing to its maturation throughout the world more than the nation of Scotland. For over two-thousand years the Highland games have been host to competitions of elite strength and skill. The first three distinguished disciplines that will be discussed are classified under the category of Track & Field, Shot Put, the Hammer Throw, and the Weight Throw. All three of these disciplines have appeared at one time or another on the modern schedule of Olympic events.

The earliest recorded accounts that resemble a modern-day Shot Put competition can be traced to the Middle-Ages when Scottish soldiers hurled or put cannonballs and stones. The first recorded modern Shot Put competition took place as part of the British Amateur Championship in 1866. The Shot Put has been included in modern Olympic competition since the inaugural games of 1896 held in Athens, Greece. Robert Garnett of Baltimore County, Maryland, was the first Shot Put gold medal winner of the modern Olympiad. It was not until the Olympics of 1948 in London, when women were given the permission to compete in Shot Put competitions.

The first woman to be awarded a gold medal for Shot Put in the Olympics was Micheline Ostermeyer of France. During that same Olympics she also won a gold medal in Discus throw and a bronze medal in High Jump. The Olympics of 1948 was also the first Olympiad with a complete Track & Field event schedule for women.

The origins of the Hammer Throw date back to the late thirteenth and early fourteenth centuries where in the Highlands hammers were commonly used for building fences to hold in sheep. It soon transformed into a measure of pure strength as a competitions during the Highland Games. The Hammer Throw first became an Olympic event during the second modern Olympiad in 1900 held in Paris, France. The first Olympic competition consisted of five throwers from two countries, the United States and Sweden, with the gold medal being presented to John Flanagan, representing the United States. He was born in Kilbreedy, County Limerick, Ireland, Thursday 9 January 1873, and immigrated to New York City in 1896 at the age of twenty-three. Women were granted permission to compete in Hammer Throw for the first time during the 2000, Olympics held in Sydney, Australia. The first female gold medal winner was Kamila Skolimowska of Poland.

The Weight Throw competition is the least internationally popular of the three sports. Its origins derive centuries ago as a cornerstone athletic event of the Highland games. Weight Throw was included on the Olympic calendar only twice. The first time was in 1904, at the Olympics held in St. Louis and then again in 1920, at the

Olympics held in Antwerp, Belgium. Six athletes from two nations, Canada and the United States, participated in the inaugural competition of the 56lb. Weight Throw. The gold medal that day was awarded to E´tienne Desmarteau of Boucherville, Quebec, Canada.

Though it might not be included in Olympic Completion anymore, it still survives as an integral part of the USA Track & Field Indoor Championships and the NCAA Men and Women Indoor and Outdoor Championships.

Curling team, Dawson, Yukon, Canada, ca. 1906.
"Public Domain. Copyright has expired, in the United States because it was
published (or registered with the U.S. Copyright office) before January 1, 1923.

Sanquhar Curlers.
"Courtesy of Dumfries Museum."

## Curling:

The root of the word curling derives from the sound resonating off the stone when it is in motion. The origins of the sport date back to medieval Scotland where brutal winter months brought the ideal conditions for this curious frozen recreation. Its first appearance in printed word can be found in a book written around 1540. In the book, John McQuhin a notary from Paisley wrote of a competition of pushing flat stones across an icy pond between a monk from Paisley Abby, Renfrewshire, named John Sclater and Gavin Hamilton. Evidence has also been substantiated of Curling's origins with the discovery of two Curling stones at the bottom of an old pond in Dunblaine dating back to 1511 and 1551. The earliest visual evidence of the sport can be found in wintery scenic paintings of Pieter the Elder Bruegel dating to around 1560. The first official Curling Club was formed in 1716, in Kilsyth, considered the birthplace of Curling. To this day the Kilsyth Curling Club is still in operation in the town. The home of the International governing body, The World Curling Federation, is located in Perth. The 1998, Winter Games in Nagano, Japan, marked the first time in modern Olympic history where Curling was placed on the Olympic calendar. During those games, Switzerland brought home the gold medal in the men's category. While Canada brought home the gold in the women's category.

In 2006, the IOC, International Olympic Committee, decided to retroactively recognize the Curling competition held during the inaugural Winter Olympics held in Chamonix, France, 1924, as the first official Olympic Curling competition.

The official name of the inaugural Winter Games was the International Winter Sports Week, thought it actually ran for eleven days. Previously Curling was plainly categorized as a demonstration sport, a lesser category of events. The first nation to bring home an Olympic gold medal was the unrivaled Great Britain team. The entire roster was comprised of Scottish born athletes from the Royal Caledonian Curling Club: William Jackson of Lamington, South Lanarkshire. He was the President of the Royal Caledonian Curling Club from 1933-1934 and father of Laurence Jackson. Robin Welsh of Edinburgh. Thomas Murray of Biggar, South Lanarkshire. Murray was the President of the Royal Caledonian Curling Club from 1936-1937, and Laurence Jackson of Carnwath, South Lanarkshire. The 1928, Winter Olympic Games held in St. Maritz, Switzerland. This was the first time the Winter Olympics was considered a separate entity from the Summer Olympic Games.

The world's first Curling Championships were held at Falkirk and Edinburgh in 1959. The first three Scotch Cup Championships were held between Canada and Scotland, with Canada capturing the first six championships. Canada owns thirty-four World Curling Championships in total. The first Women Championship was held in Perth in 1979. The winning team during the inaugural contest was Switzerland.

Public Domain.

"Courtesy of John George Brown Artist. *Curling;--a Scottish Game, at Central Park* This work is in the public domain in the United States because it was published before January 1, 1923."

Football.

Courtesy of Brian Elsey and www.historyworld.co.uk."

## Football:

Football is undoubtedly the most popular sport throughout the world. It is estimated over two billion people worldwide watch the World Cup every four years. While it is estimated more than two hundred fifty million people throughout the world are actively involved in organized football leagues in over two hundred countries worldwide. Though it is believed by some the game of Football originated in England during the 1860's, there is substantial evidence that the world's most celebrated game originated slightly north two hundred thirty years prior in Scotland. The name Fute-Ball has been used to describe games played in Scotland since the Middle-Ages. Though those games do not resemble the game of Football or Soccer played today. During its infancy, the ball was predominately carried by hand by teams of unequal sides with no kicking involved. These games of the Middle-Ages resembled more the modern-day game of Rugby or Mob Ball rather than Football.

Resulting from the rowdiness of these games numerous efforts were attempted to ban these various types of Fute-Ball games. Beginning in medieval times, 1314 until about 1667, England periodically attempted to impose bans on football games with their ban on Mob Ball. England did not possess a standing army until the seventeenth century. Subsequently during the reign of King Edward III of England in the late fourteenth century all ball games were banned throughout the empire due to the belief the public was becoming too distracted and not concentrating on their archery training.

163

Ensuing monarchs continued the embargo during their own reigns of the crown, King Richard II in 1389, King Henry IV in 1401, King Henry VII 1540, among others. The outlawing of football games also spread to France, imposed by Philip V in 1319 and King Charles V in 1369. Even in its birthplace, the Kingdom of Scotland imposed her ban. King James I in 1424, through the reign of King James IV outlawed the game of Fute-Ball due to it being too rough in motive. During the sixteenth and seventeenth century, the Puritan communities of Scotland attempted to curtail the play of Fute-Ball and ease its subsequent violent outbursts and disruptions by prohibiting boisterous ball play on the Sabbath. In 1656, the Scottish Parliament even passed an act outlawing it outright, though inevitably the authorities found themselves with a law painful to enforce. Evidence of Fute-Balls popularity is revealed in the trappings of the prevailing literature of the time. In 1636, a schoolteacher from Aberdeen named David Wedderburn, penned a Latin textbook titled *Vocabula*, describing several essential elements of the game as we know it today such as a goal keeper and passing of the ball. One of the first times the word Foot-Ball was ever penned to paper occurred in 1608 when William Shakespeare published the play King Lear, "Nor tripped neither, you base football player." (Act 1, Scene 4)

In 1906, the ban set-forth by King James I and the Scottish Parliament in 1424 outlawing the play of Fute-Ball was finally repealed. The punishment if sacked committing such an indecorous offence was a fine of four pence, though not enforced for centuries.

The first Olympic gold medal winning team in Football was none other than the Kingdom of Great Britain in 1900, Paris, France, represented by Upton Park F.C.

On St. Andrews Day 30 November 1872, the first International Football match was played. Scotland hosted England at the West of Scotland Cricket's Club ground Hamilton Crescent, Partick, Glasgow in front of a crowd of around four-thousand fans to a nil-nil draw. Scotland is also host to the world's oldest national trophy, the Scottish Cup. Another first that originated in Scotland is the usage of the term "football club" to refer to a grouping of organized ball players. The first time this occurred was around 1824-1841 in Edinburgh.

First International Football match 1872.

Andrew Watson with the Scottish team that played England at Hampden Park on the 11 March 1882.

**Andrew Watson:**

The first black athlete to play International Football.

It is said the measure of a man's true character can best be found on the athletic field, where as on the athletic field our social differences can be put aside for the pursuit of victory.

Andrew Watson was born in Demerara, British Guiana, on Saturday 24 May 1856. His father's name was Peter Miller Watson, a wealthy sugar planter born in Scotland. His father's name was James Watson, born in Crantit, Orkney, Scotland. Andrew's mother's name was Anna Rose-Watson. She was born in British Guiana. At fourteen years of age young Andrew attended the exclusive King's College School in London. At the age of nineteen he began to matriculate at the University of Glasgow where he attended natural philosophy, mathematics and engineering classes. While a student at these prestigious institutions his athletic prowess on the football pitch soon was revealed for the first time. Soon after this period he began his career in professional football. The first professional football club he joined was Maxwell FC out of Glasgow. In 1876, he then joined the Parkgrove FC. As a member of Parkgrove he was also appointed their match secretary. This is considered the first time a black man held an administration position with a professional sports club. In 1880-81, he went onto play for the preeminent powerhouse of Scottish Premier Football the Queen's Park FC. In the Scottish Cup Finals that year Queen's Park defeated Dumbarton by the score 3-1.

This was Watson's first Scottish Cup victory and the fifth for Queen's Park. This was also the first time a black man captained his team to victory in a major football competition. The following year Queen's Park once again defeated Dumbarton in the finals this time by a score of 4-1. Andrew then moved on to play for the now-defunct London Swifts in the years 1882-83. While playing with the Swifts he became the first black athlete to play in the English FA Cup. After three years playing for teams in England, the Full Back once again joined up with Queen's Park for another championship run in 1885. In the finals of that season Queen's Park defeated Renton 3-1 to capture their eighth Scottish Cup title and Watson's third. In 1881 and 1882 he also captained the Scottish National Team three times and in those three matches Scotland emerged victorious against international adversaries, twice against England and once against Wales. On 12 March 1881 Andrew Watson became the first black footballer to compete, captain and win an international football match when Scotland defeated England at The Surrey Cricket Grounds, The Oval, Kennington, London by the score 6-1. Scotland's victory that day remains the greatest lopsided football defeat England has ever suffered on their home soil. It took the United States half way through the twentieth century to racially integrate all their professional sports, though in Scotland this measure of true human equality occurred almost seventy years earlier in 1881. Unlike in the United States the issue of racial segregation was never much of a concern in Scotland.

As quoted in the minutes by a Scottish Football Association vice president prior to a match in which Watson was unable to play due to injury, "The colour of his skin was of no significance to his peers and there is no historical record of racism on the part of the Scottish Football Association."

After his playing days accounts of Watson's life are vague at best. Records show he lived in Liverpool where he qualified as a marine engineer in 1892. While some accounts state he and his family moved to London to pursue a career in engineering. There are also records illustrating he was employed as a second engineer on passenger ocean liners traveling from Glasgow to Bombay. While other accounts detail after he retired as an engineer he moved to Australia where he died in Sidney in 1902 at the age of forty-four. The last recorded document Andrew Watson's name appeared on was the marriage certificate of his son Rupert in 1915. On the document it stated his father and mother were deceased. Other accounts detail he died of pneumonia at 88 Forest Road in Kew, a suburb of London, on Tuesday 8 March 1921 at the age of sixty-four.

Andrew Watson is ranked as one of the most important footballers of the nineteenth century. But this football pioneer should also be remembered as an athletic trailblazer paving the way for racial equality throughout the world, as well as an extraordinary gentleman and teammate throughout his lifetime.

Golf.

Courtesy of Brian Elsey and www.historyworld.co.uk."

# Golf:

Games utilizing a stick and ball have been played for centuries around the world, however the modern game played over eighteen holes is strictly Scottish. Golf has been played throughout Scotland since the Middle-Ages. During its infancy golfers would knock around hard wooden balls with wooden clubs. These early wooden balls would often crack and warp, rarely traveling very far. The first written mention of the word Gowf can be traced to the 1452 decree issues by King James II and the Scottish Parliament, banning the play of Gowf and Fute-Ball. As King Edward III before him, he felt the two activities were distractions to his subjects and sidetracked them from their ever important archery training. Luckily the prohibition was lifted fifty years later by King James IV, when he gained the fondness for the sport. Further proof from antiquity of its existence is evident in the Latin textbook penned by David Wedderburn, titled *Vocabula* in 1636. The title of the section pertaining to Golf was called "Baculus", Latin for stick or club. Cited within the chapter is the term Golf hole.

The first written rules for the game of Golf were drawn up in Edinburgh, 1744. Thirteen articles were set forth for the world's first Open Golf competition by the Gentlemen Golfers of Edinburgh, later to be known as the Honourable Company of Edinburgh Golfers. Scotland also hosted the world's first professional Golf Championship. The first Open was played at Prestwick Golf Club on 17 October 1860. It was named the Open due to the fact participation was open to professionals and amateurs to compete.

The inaugural Open Championship was Willie Parks of Musselburgh. With the score of 174, Parks topped Old Tom Morris the builder of the course by two strokes that day. During the first championship the tournament was restricted solely to professionals. The following year amateurs were granted permission to play. Willie Parks later went on to win three more Open Championships, 1863, 1866 and 1875.

The Old Course at St. Andrews which dates as far back as 1574, is the most famous Golf course in the entire world and is a must visit for any Golf appreciado. Nestled comfortably within the Auld Grey Toun, lies the birthplace of the modern game. It is widely agreed by enthusiasts throughout the world very little in life compares to St. Andrews history, aura and spirit. The Links at St. Andrews are a publically owned entity controlled by the St. Andrews Links Trust. This consortium is a non-profit organization created by an Act of Parliament to oversee the management and preservation of the Links. Another responsibility of theirs is to preserve and promote a sense of accessibility and availability of the course to people of all walks of life. Though there is a waiting list to play the course, entry is much more streamlined and accessible compared to their posh counter-parts. People from all walks of life and ability can be witnessed testing their skills in all types of weather throughout the year on the course.

St. Andrews has also shared time on the silver-screen. The West Sands were the location of the opening scene in the 1981 film Chariots of Fire, winner of the Academy Award for Best Picture among three other Academy Awards that year. In the opening scene the 1924 Olympic, 400 metres gold medal winner Eric Liddell is running with his fellow potential British Olympians on the cold sands of St. Andrews shore. Golf has also been considered an Olympic sport twice in history of the games, in 1900 when the Olympics was held in Paris, France and in 1904 when the Olympics was held in St. Louis, Missouri. The first Golf gold medals were won by the United States, in the Gentleman's category Charles Sands and in the Ladies category, Margaret Abbott.

On every corner of the earth millions and millions of people today are enjoying playing Golf thanks to the Scottish.

Jim McCormick.

"Courtesy of the Benjamin K. Edward Collection, the Library of Congress and Nevada Antiques and Collectibles LLC."

## Jim McCormick

3, November 1856 – 10, March 1918

As the pages of time turn through the centuries some athletes become lost to obscurity, so can be said of Jim McCormick. He was the first man born in Scotland to play Professional baseball in the United States.

The story of this 19th century, handle bar mustached pitcher begins on a Monday in Glasgow, Scotland 3 November 1856. At the age of twenty he was offered a professional baseball contract with the Columbus Buckeyes of the International League, a professional minor league. By the next year he was pitching for the Indianapolis Browns of the National League: the Major Leagues. The first game he pitched in the big leagues was on the 20th of May 1878.

When Jim started his professional baseball career there was only six teams in the National League compared to fifteen today. In those days it was common for teams to only keep two or possibly three pitchers on the roster during the season. With most pitchers completing the games they started. Positions such as the eighth inning specialist, the set-up man, lefty specialist, middle reliever, long reliever, and the closer were all pitching categories not yet needed or even imagined in the game of baseball. The professional game of baseball that was played in the nineteenth century was slightly different to the game played today. For instance in the years 1879-1881, the National League had a rule called the foul-bound rule. This rule stated a batter could be called out if a batted ball bounced once then was caught by a fielder.

The derivative of this rule probably can be draw from the fact defensive players in the nineteenth century did not wear gloves while on the field as do modern players. There also was a rule that a batter was not granted first base if the batter was struck by a pitched ball. The reason for this rule probably derived from the fact that until 1884 pitchers in professional baseball were allowed to pitch underhand to the plate. This could also explain the exorbitant amount of innings pitched, games pitched and consequently wins accumulated by starting pitchers of the eighteen hundreds. Back then it was not out of the norm to see five hundred or even six hundred innings tallied by a starting pitcher in a single season, while these days if a pitcher tallies a mere two hundred innings in a given season he would be considered the Ace of the staff. During McCormick's professional career the bruising Scotsman pitched more than 500 innings in a season five times in ten year. In 1880, as a member of the Cleveland Blues he managed to accumulate 657.2 innings pitched. This was McCormick's high water mark of production as a professional hurler. It should also be recognized how tremendous a feat this is to accomplish. A pitching staff's Aces in the modern game would take about three seasons or possibly more to accumulate that amount of production. Even in the last year of his professional career when most athletes' production numbers tend to decline he logged in 322.1 innings pitched. While present day starting pitchers pitch every fourth or fifth day with a side practice sessions on off days, in the nineteenth century the off day for a starting pitcher was spent patrolling the outfield or some other defensive position.

176

Jim spent his "days off" corralling fly balls in the outfield while collecting 491 career hits. It is said the burly right-hander would deliver his repertoire of pitches consisting of a hard fastball, curve and a riseball that was considered more dominant than any thrown by his peers, while all being delivered with a low sidearm or underhand motion. On the mound victories came at a frequent pace for McCormick. As a member of the 1885 National League Pennant winning Chicago White Stockings pitching staff he compiled twenty victories in the regular season and all three of his teams World Series victories. The following season he topped his prior year achievements. As a member of the 1886 National League Pennant winning White Stockings he ran off sixteen straight victories in a row, while amassing thirty-one regular season victories.

Here are some of his gaudy Major League Pitching statistics:
*40 wins in a season: 2 times
*30 wins in a season: 4 times
*20 wins in a season: 8 times
*Lead the National League in Victories two times: 1880 & 1882.
*Lead the National League in Earned Run Average: 1883 & 1884.
*Lead the National League in Games pitched and Games started: 1880 & 1882.
*Lead the National League in Complete Games pitched: 1880, 1881 & 1882.
*Lead the National League in innings pitched: 1880 & 1882.
*Lead the National League in Winning Percentage: 1883.

* Lead the Union Association in Shutouts: 1884.

* Lead the National League in Fielding Percentage by a Pitcher: 1884 & 1885.

* Lead the National League in Assists by a Pitcher: 1882.

* Lead the National League in Putouts by a Pitcher: 1879 & 1882.

* Lead the National League in Batters faced by a Pitcher: 1880 & 1882.

* Highest WAR for Pitchers in the Majors: 1880 & 1882.

* The only Mayor Leaguer in the history of baseball to pitch over 500 innings in a single season five times: 1879, 1880, 1881, 1882 & 1884.

* His teams were also shut out in 43 of his 214 career losses: 20%.

* The Cleveland Blues all-time leader in pitching victories with 174.

* Roster member of every Cleveland Blues team 1879-1884.

* First base hit by a Scottish born major leaguer: 1879.

*Member of the National League Pennant winning Chicago White Stockings (presently called the Cubs): 1885- 1886.

*Pitched 10 seasons in the Major Leagues. Total of 265 Victories.

Several of the long forgotten Major League baseball clubs Jim McCormick was a member of during his profession career.

Indianapolis Browns

Cleveland Blues

Cincinnati Outlaw Reds

Providence Grey's

Chicago White Stockings (Cubs)

Pittsburgh Allegheny's (Pirates)

Hugh Nicol.

Personal Collection.

Hugh Nicol.

"Courtesy of the Benjamin K. Edward Collection, the Library of Congress and Pink Iceberg LLC."

## Hugh Nicol

Born on 1 January 1858, Campsie, Stirling, Scotland
Died on 27 June 1921, Lafayette, IN.

If the name Jim McCormick has been lost from popular memory, what can be said for the second Scottish born athlete to play professional baseball in the Major League, Hugh Nicol?

Hugh Nicol was born on Friday New Years Day 1858, in Campsie, Stirling, Scotland to Robert and Mary Nicol. As a child he and his immediate family immigrated to the United States and settled in Rockford Illinois. This first generation Scotsman immigrant found his niche in the new world on the baseball diamond. Pro scouts soon recognized his athletic prowess speeding around the bases and patrolling around the outfield grass. Soon the self proclaimed strongest 5'4" man in America was signing a professional contract with a big league ball club, the Cap Anson's White Stockings of Chicago. On 3 May 1881, at twenty-three years of age Nicol broke into the big leagues as the youngest member of the Chicago White Stockings. His first two seasons in the National League were spent as a member of a Pennant winning Championship team: 1881 and 1882. These were the days prior to the World Series. Nicol also appeared on two other Pennant winning rosters for the St. Louis Browns of the American Association in 1885 and 1886. The Browns won the World Series in 1886 against Jim McCormick's Chicago White Stockings, four games to two. This was the only time an American Association team beat a National League team in the Fall Classic.

He was unfortunately not placed on the active roster due to his low production at the plate that year.

Some of Hugh Nicol's accolades, achievements and firsts:

*Major Leagues All Time single season Stolen Base Leader: 138 in 1887.
*First Home Run hit by a Scottish born athlete in the major leagues: 9, June 1882.
*Lead the American Association in Games played: 1885 with 112.
*Lead the American Association in Outfield Assists: 1883 & 1884.
*His league leading 48 Outfield Assists in 1884 were the second most in a single season All Time.
*He is also considered the first Major Leaguer to ever slide head first into a base in a big league game.
*Involved in the first trade of two athletes in Major League history: 12, November 1886.

Most baseball enthusiasts would answer with the name Ricky Henderson if asked who holds the record for the most stolen bases in a single season. But they would be incorrect. Hugh Nicol's 138 stolen bases in 1887 top Rickey Henderson's 130 in 1981. Though it must be noted prior to 1898 the rule for accumulating stolen bases was slightly different than it is in the modern game. If a base runner was on first base and the next batter singled, then if that lead runner circled the bases and ended up on third base he would be credited with a stolen base for advancing past second to third base. He was also involved in the first trade of two athletes in the Major Leagues. On 12 November 1886 Hugh Nicol of the Saint Louis Brownstockings was traded to the Cincinnati Red Stockings for Rookie Jack Boyle.

After his big league career was over he spent six more seasons playing then managing in some obscure minor leagues throughout the country. Playing then managing for teams such as the Rockford Red Sox, Peoria Distillers, the Rock Island Islanders of the Illinois-Indiana-Iowa League, the St. Joseph Saints and the Rockford Forest City Reds of the Western Association, must have felt a million miles away from the big leagues but this experience would become invaluable in later years. He managed in the Minor Leagues from 1894-1905, winning the 1902, Three I League Championship. From 1901-1905, he also owned a minor league team in his home town of Rockford Illinois. In 1906, he became the first Athletic Director for Purdue University. Prior to his hiring all athletic matters were handled by the students with facility assistance. In his new position as athletic director, he was able to utilize all his prior managerial and championship pedigree. For the first time in the history of the University the athletic department was profitable. He also coached the Boilermakers baseball team from 1906-1914, winning the Big Ten Championship in 1909. He also developed physical education classes for students and facility emphasizing on swimming. He also developed the first inter-class sports program at the University, a prelude to an Intramural sports program. As gratitude for his tireless work at Purdue, he was honored by the 1908 graduation class with a commemorative class hat and corduroys.

Lawrence Tynes

Personal Collection.

**Lawrence Tynes**

Born: 3 May 1978 Greenock, Scotland

National Football League Placekicker 2004-present, New York Giant 2007-2013.

As rare as it is for someone to be put into the position to propel a professional football team into the Super Bowl, Lawrence Tynes had this rare opportunity bestowed upon him twice in his lifetime and on both occurrences he and his team prevailed.

Lawrence Tynes first opportunity occurred on Sunday 20 January 2008. After two unexpected victories over the Tampa Bay Buccaneers and the NFC's #1 seed and hated rivals Dallas Cowboys, the Giants traveled to Green Bay Wisconsin to face the 13-3 NFC North Division winning Packers in the NFC Championship Game with the winner advancing to Super Bowl XLII. The elements were not too inviting for either team that day. The temperatures barely tipping over minus seven degree Fahrenheit, negative twenty-one degrees Celsius, with wind chills ranging between negative twenty-seven to negative twenty-four degrees Fahrenheit, negative thirty-one degrees Celsius. To say it mildly conditions did not favor a productive kicking day. This game is considered the coldest playoff game ever played at Lambeau Field and the fifth coldest game in NFL history. Experts will always remind you of Tynes two misses that cold night in Green Bay but it should also be noted Tynes did hit three field goals in those frozen conditions that wintery night.

The stage was set. Time was ticking away in the seesaw contest. The score was deadlocked 20-20 in overtime with 12:25 remaining on the clock when the Giants field goal unit ran onto the field. As could be expected after Tynes last two misses from 43 yards and 36 yards away that would have already won the game for the Giants, confidence was not high on the New York sideline or in my living room that night. But on that night Tynes' kick went up into the Wisconsin air and right through the uprights for a 47 yard field goal and a trip to Super Bowl XLII with a final score of 23-20. With this kick Tynes set the record for the longest field goal by an opponent in a playoff game at Lambeau Field. It also marked the first time the Green Bay Packers lost a NFL/NFC championship game at home. Ironically enough his victory kick also came exactly seventeen years to the day after Matt Barr kicked the winning field goal in the 1991 NFC Championship game that propelled the New York Giants passed the San Francisco 49'ers and onto a Super Bowl XXV victory over the Buffalo Bills. Lawrence Tynes and his golden leg did not stop there. Two weeks later he kicked the first and last points: a field goal and an extra point, in the New York Giants Super Bowl victory over the New England Patriots, 17-14. With the Giant victory that day Lawrence Tynes became the first Scottish born athlete to be a member of a winning NFL Super Bowl team.

Most professional athletes would consider this moment the pinnacle to ones career but not this lad from Greenock. Lighting would strike twice for Lawrence. The stage was set on the rain drenched field at Candlestick Park, San Francisco, California, on Sunday

186

22 January 2012. After defeating the Atlanta Falcons and the Green Bay Packers in the first two rounds of the playoffs the New York Football Giants traveled to face the 13-3 NFC West Division winning San Francisco 49'ers in the NFC Championship game. At the end of regulation the game was again deadlocked and heading into overtime with the score 17-17. With 7:06 on the play clock Lawrence Tynes once again ran out onto the field and this time kicked a 31 yard field goal defeating the 49'ers by the score of 20-17 and propelled his New York Giants into Super Bowl XLVI, where they defeated the New England Patriots once again by the score 21-17.

With that kick Lawrence Tynes became the first NFL player to kick his team into two Super Bowls that his team eventually won. In addition he became the only Scottish born NFL player to be apart of two winning Super Bowl teams.

Bobby Thomson.

## Robert "Bobby" Thomson #23 New York Giants

25 October 1923- 16 August 2010

Shot Heard Around The World!

Bobby Thomson's story begins on Thursday 25 October 1923, in Glasgow, Scotland. At the age of two his father James sent for his mother Elizabeth and five other siblings to join him in New York City. The Thomson family then settled in Staten Island, a borough in New York City. This was where the New York Giants first scouted young Bobby while playing for the Curtis High School baseball team.

Now fast forward to 1951. After finishing with identical regular season win-lose records of 96-53, the Brooklyn Dodgers and the New York Giants met in a best of three game playoff series to determine the National League Champion. The first game of the series was held at Ebbets Field, the Dodgers home field. While the second and if necessary a third game was scheduled to be held at the Polo Grounds, the home field for the Giants. The boys' from Coogan's Bluff were victorious in Game One by the score of 3-1. Game Two was won by Brooklyn by a score of 10-0.

So the stage was set for Bobby's brush with immortality. On 3 October 1951, the Dodgers of Brooklyn and the Giants of Manhattan were all rapped up in a sudden death playoff series to determine the National League Champion. In the third and deciding game in the bottom of the ninth inning the score was four to one in favor of the Bums.

Alvin Dark the Short Stop for the Giants led off the inning with a single.
Then Right Fielder Don Mueller hit a single past the Dodger First
Baseman Gil Hodges that moved Alvin Dark to third. Next to bat was
Left Fielder Monte Irving whom that year led the National League in
Runs Batted In (RBI). He popped the first pitch he saw for the first out of
the inning. Then First Baseman Whitey Lockman stepped to the plate.
He hit a double scoring Alvin Dark from third. This hit untimely
knocked the Dodgers starting pitcher Don Newcombe out of the game.
On the play the Giants Don Mueller sliding into third broke his ankle and
had to be carried off the field. So with the score four to two, Lockman on
second and Clint Harting now on third and one out, the Dodgers called
upon Ralph Branca to toe the rubber and close the door on the Giant
rally. Up to bat next for the Giants was their Right Fielder Bobby
Thomson, the Staten Island Scot, for a chance to win the National
League title for the home team and a date with immortality. The Dodgers
hurler's first pitch cut the plate in half, Fastball, Strike! His next pitch
unfortunate for him will forever be remembered in baseball folklore.
Thomson connected and yanked it high and over the seventeen foot left
field wall of the Polo Grounds for a Home Run. It would be forever
known as the Miracle at Coogan's Bluff, the Shot Heard Around the
World!

Russ Hodges the Giants radio broadcaster in 1951 is forever linked to
this moment with his WMCA-AM call of the event, "There's a long
drive…..Its gonna be, I believe…..The Giants Win the Pennant!!! The
Giants Win the Pennant!!!!!

Of all the Home Runs ever hit in a professional baseball game this Home Run by the Staten Island Scot has become the defining moment of the golden age of baseball. Years later as baseball memorabilia collecting became so popular the search for the actual baseball has become one of the most sought after collectibles in the world. Some experts believe if the baseball was able to be authenticated it could be worth upwards of three million dollars.

References:

Bankston, John, *Alexander Fleming and the Story of Penicillin*, Mitchell Lane Publishers, 2002

Birch, Beverley, *Alexander Fleming, Pioneer with Antibiotics,* Blackbirch Press, 2002.

Blaise, Clark, *Time Lord: Sir Sanford Fleming and the Creation of Standard Time,* Vintage Books, 2002.

Brown, Rev. Thomas, *Memoir by the Rev. Thomas Brown 1883-4,* Obituary notice in the Edinburgh Medical Journal for Dr. Alexander Woods, Edinburgh, pg. 973-6, 1886.

Campbell, Swinton, A.A., *"Scientific Progress and Prospects" (Presidential Address to the Rontgen Society),* Nature, Vol.88, pg 191-195, 1911.

Carpenter, K.J., *The History of Scurvy and Vitamin C*, Cambridge University Press, Cambridge, 1986.

Foreman, Kenneth E., Husted, Virginia M., *Track and Field, Physical Education Activities Series,* WM. C. Brown Company Publishers, 1966.

Goodfellow, James, OBE., *History of the ATM, 1965-67. The Coded Token &PIN, The Access System of all today's ATMs, Cash Dispensers and POS Terminals.* March 2008.

Grolier Educational, *The Grolier Library of Science Biographies, Volume 6 & 3*, Grolier Educational, Danbury, Connecticut 1997.

Hall, Henry, *American Successful Men on Affairs. An Encyclopedia of Contemporaneous Biography Volume 1.*, The New York Tribune, 1895 pg. 119.

Harlow, Alvin F., *Andrew Carnegie*, Julian Messner, New York 1953.

Hills, Adrian, *"Eye of the World; John Logie Baird and Television: Part I,"* Kinema, No.5, pg5, 1996.

Kamm, Anthony, Baird, Malcolm H., *John Logie Baird: A Life.* National Museums of Scotland, Enterprise Limited, 2002.

"It was Goodfellow who came up with the idea of a four-digit PIN which would allow people to access their cash". The Scotsman. 15 September 2007. Retrieved 17 January 2010.

James, Bill, & Neyer, Rob, *The Neyer/ James Guide To Pitchers, An Historical Compendium of Pitching, Pitchers, and Pitches.* Fireside, Simon & Schuster, Inc, 2004.

Jarow, Jesse, *Telegraph and Telephone Networks. Groundbreaking Developments in American Communications.* Rosen Classroom, Primary Source. Rosen Classroom Books & Materials, New York, 2004

Maurois, Andre, *The Life of Sir Alexander Fleming. Discoverer of Penicillin*, E.P. Dutton & Company, Inc., New York 1959.

Moseley, Sydney A., *John Baird...The Romance and Tragedy of the Pioneer of Television*, Odhams Press, London, 1952.

Natural International Weekly Journal of Science, *Obituary of Alexander Muirhead*, Nature, 106, pg. 668-669. 20 Jan. 1921.

Panati, Charles, Extraordinary Origins of Everyday Things, Harper & Row, Publishers, New York, 1987.

Paschoff, Naomi, *Alexander Graham Bell Making Connections,* Oxford University Press, New York, Oxford, 1996

Perry, David B., *Bike Cult, The Ultimate Guide to Human-Powered Vehicles,* Four Walls Eight Windows, New York/London, 1995.

Pridmore, Jay and Hurd, Jim, *The American Bicycle,* Motorbooks International Publishers & Wholesalers, Osceola, WI, 1995.

Purdue University Libraries, Archives and Special Collections. Hugh Nicol collection, Obituary found in his faculty folder.

Rinaldi, Giancarlo, *Kirkpatrick Macmillan: 200th Anniversary of a man who pioneered pedal cycles.* News South Scotland, 1 September 2012.

Schuman, Michael A., *Alexander Graham Bell Inventor and Teacher*, Enslow Publications, Inc., Berkeley Heights, NJ. 1999.

195

Simon, Charles May, *The Andrew Carnegie Story*, E.P. Dutton & Company, Inc., New York 1965.


Simon & Goodman Picture Co. Production, *The American Experience, "The Telephone"*, WGBH Educational Foundation, 1997.


Stepanek, Sally, *World Leaders Past and Present Mary Queen of Scots*. Chelsea House Publishers, Philadelphia, 1987.


Stockton, Frank R., *Round-About Rambles in Lands of Fact and Fancy.* Scribner, Armstrong & Co., New York, 1872.


Tiltman, R.F., Radio News. (1928, November). How "Stereoscope" Television is Shown. *Bairdtelevision.*
http://www.bairdtelevision.com/stereo.html


The Times (London). (1926, January). The "Televisor" Successful Test of New Apparatus. *Bairdtelevision.* http://
www.bairdtelevision.com/firstdemo.html

Wood, A, *"A New Method for Treating Neuralgia by the Direct Application of Opiates to Painful Points",* Edinb. Med. Surg. J., 82:265-81, 1855.